the
SECRET
COUNTRY of
YOURSELF

Jean— I hope you find
solace + inspiration in
these pages..

many blessings on
your Path—

Jenya
'17

About the Author

Jenya T. Beachy has been an active member of the Santa Cruz, California, community for more than twenty years, and she's served on the Redwood Circles Council and the Board of Community Seed Earth-Spirit Fellowship. She is also the founder of the Deep Well–Great Heart Society.

To Write to the Author

If you wish to contact the author or would like more information about this book, please write to the author in care of Llewellyn Worldwide, and we will forward your request. Both the author and the publisher appreciate hearing from you and learning of your enjoyment of this book and how it has helped you. Llewellyn Worldwide cannot guarantee that every letter written to the author can be answered, but all will be forwarded. Please write to:

Jenya T. Beachy
℅ Llewellyn Worldwide
2143 Wooddale Drive
Woodbury, MN 55125-2989

Please enclose a self-addressed stamped envelope for reply,
or $1.00 to cover costs. If outside the USA, enclose
an international postal reply coupon.

Many of Llewellyn's authors have websites with additional information and resources. For more information, please visit www.llewellyn.com.

the

SECRET
COUNTRY *of*
YOURSELF

Discover the Powerful Magic
of Your Endless Inner World

JENYA T. BEACHY

Llewellyn Publications
Woodbury, Minnesota

First Edition
First Printing, 2017

Book design by Bob Gaul
Cover design by Shira Atakpu

Llewellyn Publications is a registered trademark of Llewellyn Worldwide Ltd.

Library of Congress Cataloging-in-Publication Data
Names: Beachy, Jenya T., author.
Title: The secret country of yourself: discover the powerful magic of your
    endless inner world / Jenya T. Beachy.
Description: Woodbury: Llewellyn Worldwide, Ltd., 2017. | Includes
    bibliographical references and index.
Identifiers: LCCN 2017034516 (print) | LCCN 2017044180 (ebook) | ISBN
    9780738753744 (ebook) | ISBN 9780738752150 (alk. paper)
Subjects: LCSH: Self-actualization (Psychology)—Miscellanea. |
    Self—Miscellanea. | Self-knowledge, Theory of—Miscellanea.
Classification: LCC BF1045.S44 (ebook) | LCC BF1045.S44 B43 2017 (print) |
    DDC 158.1—dc23
LC record available at https://lccn.loc.gov/2017034516

Llewellyn Worldwide Ltd. does not participate in, endorse, or have any authority or responsibility concerning private business transactions between our authors and the public.

All mail addressed to the author is forwarded, but the publisher cannot, unless specifically instructed by the author, give out an address or phone number.

Any Internet references contained in this work are current at publication time, but the publisher cannot guarantee that a specific location will continue to be maintained. Please refer to the publisher's website for links to authors' websites and other sources.

Llewellyn Publications
A Division of Llewellyn Worldwide Ltd.
2143 Wooddale Drive
Woodbury, MN 55125-2989
www.llewellyn.com

Printed in the United States of America

Acknowledgments

$\mathcal{I}$ would like to respectfully acknowledge those folks who've helped this book come into being, directly or indirectly.

Huge, brilliant, woojie thanks to:

Matthew Beachy, my best beloved, teacher, poet, and king of my heart, I'm forever grateful for your love, your patience, and those not-so-tasty but very nutritious truth sandwiches.

Lasara Firefox Allen, for the introductions, inspiration, wild laughs, deep love. You told me I could do it and I did it!

Elysia Gallo, for taking a chance on me. Jason Mankey, who gave me the opportunity to pen a few notes for his first book, which by a weird set of circumstances led to the publishing of this one. John Mirassou, for walking beside me while Shapeshifter was being born, for being my first (and only, thus far!) initiate, and for friendship all down the line.

Cora Anderson, your initiation blessing reminded me that, yes, we are here to serve. And Victor, for opening doors leading every-witch-way. T. Thorn Coyle, for setting an example. You continue to inspire. Veedub and Diana Walker, for the sense and sensibility, the ever-boisterous circles of laughter and magick, and for opening the Starry Gate for me.

Alison Harlow, for friendship, activism, and bringing it down to earth. Francesca de Grandis, for the dark heart of poetry. I may not have been yours, but your Work shifted everything I thought I knew about the Craft. Happy-dog, for kinship in general, and the name "Shapeshifter" in particular.

Limnaia, for phrasing: "Clearly, your first language is Witch." Dakini, for the Crystal Library. All my students, who were there for the inception of the Secret Country, thank you for your openness, your commitment, your insight.

All my readers, who helped me tame this monstrosity of words/works into some sort of cohesive form.

And from a more practical standpoint, many thanks to:

Our landlords/mates, Cindy and Richard, for putting up with six months of no-chores-doing on the Farm.

My Mom and Dad, for "I've been very lucky!" and "You make your own luck!" and the marriage of these two viewpoints in me.

My children and my extended family, who have provided fodder for my greatest and most beloved lessons. I adore you all.

Preface

*T*his book is for...

The seekers and the mystics, those who can't stop finding truth everywhere: peering into the microscope, kneeling at the altar, spinning in the lodge, gazing at the stars, prostrating on the rug, dancing around the fire.

The scientists and the poets, whose search for the elegant solution is guided by their desire for beauty.

The believers, the unbelievers, the want-to-believers, the never-quite-sure.

But mostly, this book is for the curious, those for whom life (and beyond) is a great adventure meant to be engaged with a whole heart.

Blessed be your unique journey.
Blessed be the secret country of yourself.

Contents

Intro *1*

Part One—The Preparation
One: A Worthy Endeavor 7

What Is the Secret Country of Yourself? 7

What Can You Do There? 10

How Does It Work? 11

   Purging Preconceptions 14

Two: Becoming a Fit Traveler 15

Your Soul-Fire 17

   The Soul-Fire Invocation 17

The Three That Are One 19

   Your Talker 20

   Your Fetch 22

   Your Godself 24

Your Souls Aligned 26

Life-Force, the Ha Prayer, and the Rite of Untangling 27

    The Ha Prayer for Triple-Soul Alignment 28

    The Untangling Rite 31

Values and Virtues 32

    Making Your Core Values Pentacle 34

    Running Your Values Pentacle 36

Morning Practice 38

Three: Gathering the Gear 39

Your Home Base 40

The Secret Country Starter Kit 41

    Making the Altar 43

Recording for Posterity (Or Just for Yourself) 45

Your Travelogue and Map 48

    Collaging: Art for Everyone! 48

    Travelogue Pages 49

    Making the Map 50

Four: Inviting Alliances 53

Magickal Community 53

Guides and Guardians 56

    Seeking the Ally 57

Talking to Your Tools 58

Part Two—The Expedition

Five: The Sanctuary 63

Your Sacred Home 63

    Ha Prayer for Integration 67

Visiting the Sanctuary 69

Sanctuary—Head, Heart, Hands 73

Head: What Makes You Feel Safe? 73

Heart: Songs of Fulfillment and Joy 74

Hands: Sanctuary Model/Collage 74

The Gifts of Joy and Fulfillment 74

Roadblocks to Joy and Fulfillment 76

Loving-Kindness Blessing Practice 79

Loving-Kindness Gratitude Practice 82

Dreams and Visions—The Unbidden Contact 82

Memory Play 84

Dreams and Visions Exercise 85

More Magick at the Sanctuary 86

Cleansing Bath 87

Planting Intentions 89

Sending Energy from Godself to Godself 91

Six: The Shadow House 93

Meeting the Darkness 93

The Demons: Problems with Personalities 97

Visiting the Shadow House 98

Shadow House—Head, Heart, Hands 102

Head: What Scares You? 102

Heart: Whistling in the Dark 102

Hands: Shadow House Model/Collage 102

The Gifts of Courage and Compassion 103

Seeking, Hearing, Speaking 105

The Shadows of the World 107

World Shadows 109

More Magick at the Shadow House 109

A Spell for Protection 109

A Talisman for Strength 110

Bone-Deep Healing 111

Seven: The Temple 113

Worshipping Your Gods 113

Your Thoughts on God 116

The Compost of Your Past 117

Visiting the Temple 119

Temple—Head, Heart, Hands 121

Head: Do You Believe in God? 121

Heart: Praying to Small Gods 122

Hands: Temple Model/Collage 122

The Gifts of Guidance and Discernment 122

Trusting Your Intuition 126

The Hall of Tarot 126

The Arcane Journey 127

More Magick at the Temple 129

Cutting Ties Exercise 130

Most Powerful Allies 130

The Not-So-Silent Supper 131

Eight: The School 133

All Knowledge, Some Wisdom 133

Sharing Knowledge and Power 137

Visiting the School 137

School—Head, Heart, Hands 140

Head: Filling the Library with Books 140

Heart: You're Wrong! Isn't that Awesome? 140

Hands: School Model/Collage 140

The Gifts of Curiosity and Creativity 141

Thoughts vs. Thinking 144

The Library 146

Mowgli and Cerridwen 147

More Magick at the School 154

  A Spell for Clarity and Wisdom 155

  The Council of Elders 155

  Crown of Success Spell 156

Part Three—Through the Gates of Magick

Nine: The Wilderness Within You 161

  The Blessing of Your Senses 162

The Realm of Air: The High Mountains 166

  The Gift of Knowing 166

  Visiting the Realm of Air 167

  Air—Head, Heart, Hands 169

The Realm of Fire: The Desert of Shifting Sands 170

  The Gift of Will 170

  Visiting the Realm of Fire 172

  Fire—Head, Heart, Hands 174

The Realm of Water: Rivers to the Sea 175

  The Gift of Daring 175

  Visiting the Realm of Water 176

  Water—Head, Heart, Hands 178

The Realm of Earth: Forest and Field 179

  The Gift of Silence 179

  Visiting the Realm of Earth 181

  Earth—Head, Heart, Hands 183

More Magick with the Elements 184

  Meeting the Elementals 184

  A Nighttime Prayer for Protection and Good Dreams 187

Ten: Home Again, Home Again 189

The Mysteries of Birth, Life, and Death 189

The Heart of the Cosmos and the Gift of Freedom 192

Visiting the Heart of the Cosmos 193

The Heart of the Cosmos—Head, Heart, Hands 195

The Heart of the World and the Gift of Form 196

Visiting the Heart of the World 197

The Heart of the World—Head, Heart, Hands 199

The Heart of You and the Gift of Yourself 199

Visiting the Heart of Yourself 200

More Magick from the Heart 201

Child of Earth and Sky Practice 201

A Circle of Safety for Self or Stuff 201

A Song from Heart to Heart to Heart: All the Love that Flows 203

Outro 205

Appendix A: List of Values 207

Exercises, Prayers, Practices, Spells, and Rites Index 211

Bibliography 215

Intro

You walk across the deep green grass, feeling the morning dew wet on your feet and legs. The sun is warm on your shoulders. The trill of birdsong follows you as you head toward the small building that holds the keys to many a mystery. The morning is alive with possibility.

As you enter the light and airy hut, you are warmly welcomed by those already seated in a circle on the floor or in comfortable chairs. Find the best place for yourself and sit. Breathe. Center.

———————

Hello beauties, and welcome to the secret country of yourself. I will be your first teacher and guide on this wonder-filled journey into your own hidden worlds.

The secret country of yourself is your unique inner cosmos. The experiences you have there can change your life. You visit the secret country in your dreams and fantasies, your visions and imaginings.

This course of study you are embarking on includes a series of guided meditations, a tour, if you will, of some small part of this internal landscape, along with practices and magicks that support your exploration.

The purpose of this is three-fold: to know yourself, to heal yourself, to become all of who you are.

Essentially, everything of value on this expedition is already in you. It will be such an adventure to find it!

What's my story?

I've been walking the twisted path of the craft for over thirty years, much longer if you count back to my childhood, standing at the edge of the woods calling for the monsters to come out. In many ways, I am still doing that.

In my time, I've had many teachers: the cycles of moon and star, the spiral of the seasons; the pattern of breath, rising and falling and rising; leaf and root and wing and song and fear and grace. I've also had the great good fortune to share the magick circle with many powerful and wise human teachers.

I believe that each of us is here for some purpose. We are the gods that the universe invoked into the world at this time and place because we are necessary. Our task is to live according to our own deep truths, fulfilling the need of the world for our unique gifts.

I am the originator of the Shapeshifter line within the Anderson Feri Tradition of Witchcraft. My lineage incorporates concepts and practices from neo-paganism, from Jane Roberts's *Seth Material*, Buddhist teachings, Rumi's poetry, and from tending the land and the animals here at my home at Dirt-Heart Farm. I consider my first language to be Witch, but I speak others as well.

This is not a book about my lineage, but it is, of course, fey-touched. We will be using some material from Feri tradition as I learned it, the doctrine of the Three Souls in particular. We will also be using two foundational practices of the tradition, the Ha Prayer and the Untangling Rite (known in some circles as the *Kala* Rite). These are strong ways to raise, store, and send life-force energy.

These ideas came into Feri tradition from *Huna*, a metaphysical system developed by Max Freedom Long based on his (sometimes flawed) understanding of native Hawai'ian spiritual teachings. I have worked with these practices for over twenty years to great effect, folding them into my own work to create new ways of relating to self and spirit.

Though I do use the words *gods* and *spirits* throughout this course, I invite you to define them as it suits you: archetypes, living personalities, aspects of yourself. You might even consider that this is a great fantasy story, where the characters are believable and there is internal consistency. See these journeys as a (mostly) friendly trip into the place where ideas come from, or your own psychology.

Also, because little of what we do in the secret country has anything to do with gender, I will be using the singular "they" throughout this course. I may refer to Source or All-That-Is by the names God Herself and Goddess Himself. Your experience may include beings who identify as male or female or nonbinary or beyond binary or anything else on the continuum. I prefer not to create false limitations by using gendered terminology.

We are going to go to a place that is different for each traveler. I will offer you possibilities, point out hazards, and open doors. It is always up to you to step through.

You have already been to the secret country many times in your life. So why should you sign on to this particular expedition?

Come on this journey because you are a miracle, a golden child, a blessing to the worlds. The rich deliciousness of you is just waiting to be revealed, and you are too precious a resource to go undiscovered.

Come because you want a program, an itinerary, to help you navigate the strangeness you have found. Come because you want to learn how to travel better through this enchanting place.

Come because maybe your life is broken. Because you've been struggling with financial or romantic problems and you can't figure out why everything keeps going wrong.

Or maybe because your life is already amazing and you are psyched for a new adventure!

Come because you were hip-deep in a strong dream and awakened before you finished the quest. Or because you are in the middle of the biggest inspiration of your life and are having trouble clarifying the vision.

Come with me because something is calling you to a deeper understanding of yourself. Something is going unfinished, unknown, unappreciated. And that mystery won't let you rest.

The call from the secret country might sound like the voice of your gods or your ancestors telling you, "Go with Ms. Jenya, now!" If you are a diviner, your tarot cards or runes may send you clues.

Maybe you keep finding a certain word or phrase popping up in the books you read, the TV programs you watch, or the music you listen to. It might seem like just a weird coincidence. But maybe it's not that simple. What if this is the language of the unseen (within you or without)? It could be a long-forgotten dream trying to get a message across the divide between conscious and unconscious. Or your guardian angel reminding you of your destiny. I'm not sure that it's important which is more true.

As a wise philosopher once said, "The most important answer is the one you believe." (That was my husband. I had to marry a man that smart.)

I look forward to helping you find your own answers.

Part One

THE
PREPARATION

---— *One* ———

A WORTHY ENDEAVOR

Take a moment to stand and stretch, to look around at your setting. The walls are of cherry wood, polished to a smooth shine. There are tall built-in bookcases, full as they can be with all sorts of titles, the leather bindings and old paper giving off a warm smell that permeates the room. Through a door you can see a glimpse of a small kitchen, rosemary and sage and lavender hanging in bunches from the ceiling, fresh peaches in a hand-thrown bowl on the table. Make yourself easy here. Relax.

———————

What Is the Secret Country of Yourself?

It's a bright bonfire on a full-moon night.

It's a meadow shining with spring's first sunrise.

It's a river of dreams and a mountain of adversity and the greatest story never yet told.

It's an imaginary world and another dimension and a different astral plane.

I just made it up and so will you. All of these are true.

Simply put, the secret country of yourself is your personal sacred space within. Whenever you close your eyes, you are in your own secret country. Everything you experience that is not happening in the physical realm (which I like to call the *shared reality*) is happening there. Your daydreams and night dreams and wild fancies are part of it. Mythologies, ancient and modern, are part of it. When the muse calls with a song in the middle of the night, the caller ID reads "secret country." When you receive an idea for a new theorem, the return address reads "secret country." It's the birthplace of inspiration.

This is a new magickal technology that is as ancient as imagination, and it's creating itself in me and you and all who care to join us. It is a spiritual practice and a religious experience; it's a science and a craft and an art.

The secret country of yourself is secret because no one else can possibly know what happens there. The lavish landscapes, the learning/praying/dancing/loving, the unique magick that is striving to be born from you each moment ... these are the settings, the plots, the characters. The secret country is secret because there are no words to describe the entirety of what you will find.

Will you be alone? Yes. Will you never be alone? Yes. Like cells in the body of God, organisms in the ecosystem of Gaia, or notes in the music of the spheres, you are differentiated from all others, and you resonate with all others. Every bit of you has been something or someone else. It's so exciting!

But I hear you asking, "Is the secret country really-really real?"

Try this: close your eyes for a moment. See the room described at the start of this chapter. See the other folks who have come together for this teaching. See me speaking to you. You are in my classroom in the secret country in this very moment. Is it real for you?

The secret country of yourself will offer you experiences that no one else may ever see or know about. This is internal reality, and yours will not be like everyone else's. You are a singular creature, with your own gifts to give, which you gain and hone in your inner world.

Everyone's secret country is a little bit different, but there are commonalities. We all have something that passes for a home of light and darkness, a place for learning, a space for spiritual communion. We all hold within us aspects of the classical elements of air, fire, water, and earth. But this is only the beginning. The unexplored places within you are infinite, and once you learn how to navigate the terrain, you can spend the rest of your life exploring your own beauty.

All the aspects of your life are represented there: family, home, work, spirit. The institutions you love and hate in the shared reality are also within you. You will find parts of yourself that you've imprisoned, that are completing advanced degrees, that are healing other parts. There is so much more to you than you can ever know.

The secret country may be populated by your favorite fictional characters, or the gods of your religious path, or both. I encourage you to keep your eyes, your mind, and your heart open to receive wisdom in whatever form it appears. Guides and guardians from your personal traditions will help in your work. Gods, Orisha, Lwa, djinn, devas, faeries, and angels are some of the entities you may meet.

And the secret country is a living, breathing, growing place where life goes on, even when you're not actively paying attention. It has some qualities similar to the "mind palace," or what one of the characters in John Crowley's *Little, Big* describes as a "memory house," with this twist: "The greatest practitioners of the old art discovered some odd things about their memory houses the longer they lived in them … it was discovered, for instance, that the symbolic figures with vivid expressions, once installed in their proper places, are subject to subtle change as they stand waiting to be called forth … also, as the memory house grows, it makes conjunctions and vistas that its builder can't conceive of beforehand."

The characters continue their own journeys, meet each other, make connections, and gain experience. They love and fight and make music and art, which you may choose to bring forth into the physical realm. You are the doorway to your own secret country, the point where the two realities intersect.

Most importantly, the secret country is a place where you learn to become a stronger, better person wherever you go. Understanding your value, facing your fears, connecting to your gods and spirits, and seeking knowledge all help you to act more skillfully in all areas. Spending time in the wilderness inside of you gives you new respect for the planet you live on. When you bring all your experiences together, they provide a good foundation for a life lived in service to yourself and others.

Let your travels in the secret country be an inspiration to light a candle, write a letter, put your arms around a thing you love and protect it with all your fierce might.

What Can You Do There?

In the secret country of yourself, you can find what lies within yourself and what lies beyond the physical realm of yourself. You can get to the invisible heart of things and connect on a deep level. You can look for the ways that you and the world intersect, in private, where you are free to experiment. You can practice things that scare you in the shared reality: having the talk with your boss or your partner, jumping off the high-dive. You can expand what is possible for you and your world.

- You can gather resources and connect with guides and allies.

- You can reach back to your ancestors and forward to your descendants.

- You can learn to honor and celebrate yourself through your interactions with past and future selves.

- You can run the gauntlet of deep, dark spiritual practice or dance around the fire with your animal guides.

- You can experience the stillness at the center of your being.

- You can look for the things that are holding you back from the life you want for yourself.

- You can study with any teacher who has ever or never lived.

- You can read any book, written or unwritten. You can read the book you haven't written yet.

- You can meet with the gods of your heart, the gods of your people—gods you never imagined could exist.

- You can visit the realms of the elements and learn their secrets.

- You can soar to the center of the universe and burrow deep in the belly of the Earth.

And always you return to the shared reality. Maybe you have changed. Maybe everything has changed.

How Does It Work?

The secret country of yourself course includes many different practices of exploration, enjoyment, and expression. It is designed to engage your elegant mind, your delicious animal self, and the starry crown of your divinity.

In part one, we'll go through how to get ready for whatever you might find. You'll learn about staying centered and in harmony with yourself. You'll gain some tools for keeping your energy up and staying clear about what's important to you. You'll gather accoutrements and build an altar. The travelogue and map you make will serve as a record of where you've been and how you were changed by being there.

I'll tell you what I've learned of this place in my years of guiding people through it. I'll explain a bit about the locales we will visit and offer ways to connect to those places in the shared reality as well as in the inner landscape. When we are done with this section, you will have new tools and techniques to support and enrich your life, and not only in the secret country.

In part two, we embark! Here you will find background information about each place you're visiting, a guided meditation, and some suggestions for activities you can do to express the experiences you had there into the shared reality. You will also find exercises, prayers, practices, spells, and rites to help you work with these places in your daily life. Self-knowledge is awesome and even better when you turn it to practical applications!

I encourage you to dedicate at least one moon cycle, from full to full, or new to new, to each locale and really dig into it. Read through the chapter first, then schedule your meditations and exercises and honor your calendar! It's too easy to let your personal spiritual work fall by the wayside when times are busy or tough, but it's precisely then that you most need the support that a mystical practice provides.

You can work this program either alone or with others, or some of both. If you are doing this work with a group, you might take turns reading the meditations out loud. If you are doing this work alone, I encourage you to record the meditations, leaving a breath or so between sentences. This will be enough for you to sink down into the work easily. Leave space where indicated for your meanderings, and then record the final section, which brings you back safely to the shared reality. If you don't have access to a recording device or a group to work with, you can still do the meditations—it just might take a little more focus to move into the desired trance state.

There is an itinerary, of course. But it is more than a litany of locations: it's a treasure map, a scavenger hunt, a program of spiritual development. In each of these places, you will find new challenges that offer new gifts. We go in a specific order, because I have found that this gives a well-rounded experience of the secret country. There will be time to wander as you like among the marvels of your inner worlds, but we start with the basics.

Throughout these travels, we go together, but separately. Each takes the journey to their own secret country, but none of us is truly alone.

We begin with the Sanctuary, your heart's true home, where you discover the gifts of joy and fulfillment. There you will also learn to stay open to your dreams and visions: what the night can teach you, through your slumbering self, and what your mental meanderings at any time can offer.

Second, we go to visit the Shadow House. Here live all the parts of you that you've hidden away from the world, for fear they are too ugly or too beautiful. In the Shadow House, you gather the courage to listen with compassion to the stories of your pain or rage, as told by those aspects of you that are still suffering.

Then it's off to the Temple to connect with your gods, whatever form they take. Here you learn about guidance and discernment and how divination can create gateways through which you can step and learn from the archetypes there. You'll also visit the Cemetery and, if you wish, commune with your ancestors of blood and spirit.

Next, you continue your education at the School, where curiosity and creativity rule the day. You'll go to the Library, and from there, into some worlds that were created by others to see what adventures you find. Have you ever wanted to run with the wolves like Mowgli or stir the Cauldron of Cerridwen? In this section you'll practice putting yourself directly into these stories, taking the place of this character or that, and see how your understanding grows.

All of this is lovely and powerful and awfully civilized!

So next you head out (in!) to the wilderness where you connect with your elemental kin. You learn to rise above it all on the wings of air, gaining perspective on your hurts and healing. In the fire at your core, you find the transformation that allows you to move forward. From rain to river to pounding ocean, water quenches you and teaches you how to wear down or go around. Then you spend time in the realm of earth, feeling yourself solid and grounded.

Finally, you rise into the heart of the cosmos, sink to the heart of the world, and come home to the blessedness that is the heart of yourself.

Your past experiences in the shared reality can limit your experiences in all the worlds, unless you take steps to get outside those boundaries. So I encourage you to feed your secret country with images and stories that are unfamiliar. Travel! Experiment! Read gardening and photography magazines. Read novels, historical or not, and allow yourself time to explore the worlds presented there. Go to museums and look at paintings and sculptures and all manner of art. Travel to the mountains and the desert and the beach.

Each time you go forth, go with your past held lightly in you. Bring the tools you might need. And know that the words are not the only truth; the map is not the place; the finger is not the moon.

Purging Preconceptions

We can all be affected by our preconceived notions about any of these locales. It's good to know what these notions are before you start. Take a moment now to write for five minutes or so on each of these places: Sanctuary, Shadow House, Temple, School. It is not necessary to know what I mean by those words. This exercise is meant for you to discover what you think and feel about them and to give you an opportunity to challenge those ideas, if you choose.

Two

BECOMING A
FIT TRAVELER

You are called now to go to another place, a more spacious room that you hadn't noticed before. Here you find the same well-worn hardwood floors but little in the way of decor, only long trestle tables along the walls. The books are absent, and in their place, on two adjacent walls, there are mirrors. The other two walls are covered with windows, through which you can look out onto a meadow ringed by tall trees: redwood, oak, bay. You can hear the chittering of the squirrels as they scold the blue jays trying to roost too close. The sun is past its zenith. You give your attention back to the room you are in and the matter at hand.

———————

Okay, lovelies. It's time for us to get on the same page with our terms and practices. There are some basic principles that I need to share with you to ensure that we are speaking a common language. I mentioned before that my work is partly rooted in Feri practices. This is where those methods begin to come into play. Those practices, and the other things you learn in this section, will be the underpinning of all that comes next. So, even if it gets confusing or, dare I say, a teeny bit boring, stay with me! The relevance will become clear and we'll get to the good stuff in two shakes.

Of course, you may find concepts here that you don't agree with or that don't make intuitive sense to you. I encourage you to take your time and play around with these ideas. Don't get hung up over minute details. By far, the spirit of what you do in the secret country is more important than the letter. Whatever you learn or don't learn here, whatever you take away from this course, your secret country is all yours, always.

This is the part of the process when you begin to become aware of the deep magick of your own sweet self. You find the great intricacy and elegance of how you're put together and learn ways to support the growth of the parts of you that you truly admire and love. That bit is excellent. Everyone loves that bit. But now is also when issues begin to arise. Revelations of discomfort, anger, and frustration can make you just want to quit. Again, stick with it! Having all this self-knowledge under your belt will help you to be safe and make the most of your interactions in the secret country.

Remember, there are many trials in every worthy quest. The best stories teach that, if there's value in the enterprise, there are dangers on the path. Adversaries appear, obstacles arise, you get tired and feel weak. Change happens quickly and scares you and those around you, or it happens too slowly and you are tempted to go back to your comfy chair. Rather than trying to avoid these difficulties, you have the option to focus on your fitness and strengthen your resolve. That's what we're going to do in this section. But how?

First, you're going to practice getting centered in who you are. You find the unique fire of your true self and get to know it intimately.

Next, it's time to play with energy: to find it, raise it, use it. You do this through your awareness of how all your parts work together: the spiritual, physical, intellectual.

Then, it's time to really think about what is important to you. Being aware of your priorities is crucial for living a life of integrity.

Finally, I ask you to commit to an ongoing morning practice that gives you time and space to sit with yourself and be at peace. This helps immeasurably in the quest to know, heal, and fully inhabit yourself. Sticking to it reminds you that you are important and deserve to take that time.

This sounds like a lot. It is a lot. When setting out to climb Mount Everest, someone may spend years training for a trek of only a few months. But the strength of will and sense of accomplishment last a lifetime.

There are tall mountains in you, too. And immense libraries, and exquisite holy places, all for you to explore. How wonderful!

Your Soul-Fire

Everyone has a holy flame that burns at the center of their body. This flame is the star of your own true self. When it is bright and strong, you are healthy and vibrant, and vice versa. This bright sun can be fed with breath, with energy, with visualizations. This is your soul-fire, and it illuminates all it touches. It can also be used to warm or cleanse you, which we're going to practice in a moment.

We all accumulate "stuff" just walking through life: our mother's fear, our neighbor's disapproval, our boss's anger. This energetic mess can distort your view, hurt your self-esteem, and generally make you sick. The Soul-Fire Invocation will help you clean this stuff off before it really takes hold.

The Soul-Fire Invocation

Find a comfortable, quiet place. You are going to expand your belly as much as possible, so take a position that lets you do that. Standing or lying down is best, if you can.

Start with your attention in your belly. See the flicker that is in the very center of you. Spend a little time here. What does the flame look like? Yellow? Blue? How hot is it? Is it gentle like a candle flame or wild like a forest fire? Does it have a shape? A sound or fragrance? There's no need to make sense of what you experience. Just let it be and observe.

Then, breathe into that place and see the flame begin to grow and get stronger. Let its sphere of illumination begin to increase in size like a bubble being blown by your breath. See this bubble as a sort of filter expanding within you and pushing out from you the things that aren't yours. See a momentary spark in each place that your soul-fire touches something that doesn't belong to you, or that no longer serves you, and watch that something dissipate.

Let the filter of light expand with each breath you take and feel it moving out and out from you. Keep this flow going until you feel clear. If you're not sure what that feels like, that's okay. Read this prayer/poem slowly, allowing your breathing to coincide with the words; i.e., breathe in while reading "Breathe into the light in the center of you." Then breathe out while reading "Air feeds fire."

Breathe into the light in the center of you. Air feeds fire.
Breathe into the light in the center of you. You shine like the sun.
Breathe into the light in the center of you and feel the spill of stars there.
Feel the expansion and the contraction as your very flesh models the mystery:
Everything rises and falls and rises again.
Feel the sacredness of you, the wholeness. Feel the brilliance of you.
You are a star and a child of the stars!
Feel yourself full of your own soul-fire.
This is who you are when no one is asking you for anything.
This is who you are when you are not only alone, but all-one.
This is you: blood and bone and bright joy.
This is you: strong and free and beautiful.
This is you: mud and fire, brilliant consciousness hovering within and animating this entity.

Spirit inhabiting flesh for now, you are fit for this exploration.
You are made for this knowing of yourself.
Blessed be your magick.

When you are finished, draw the sphere of energy back into your belly, ready for
anytime it is needed.

The Three That Are One

Scientific and spiritual findings teach us that we are one with all things, sharing breath, molecules, energy. Yet, we are also individuated cells in the body of God (or All-That-Is or You-Are-Making-This-Up or whatever name you prefer!). As individuals, we have an opportunity to learn, change, and grow by our interactions with other people, things, and situations.

Just so, it can be helpful to consider that you are not just one soul, but three: one is the soul of the body and animates the physical form; one is the soul of the mind and sparks your intelligence; and one is the soul of your divinity, the god that is you. Together as three-in-one, along with your body, they make up the entirety of your holy presence. Each of these souls has their own gifts and challenges. By paying attention to what they want and can offer, and how they interact, you achieve a few things:

- First, you know yourself better, which is an important goal of any traveler.

- Second, you gain a greater ability to locate your hurts, so that you can heal them.

- Third, you learn to have all your parts working in concert, so that you become more effective in your life.

Many cultures have come upon the concept of multiple parts of the human etheric anatomy, and they're strikingly similar, though of course the names are different. Plato talked about a Triple Soul and compared them to three societal functions. Freud defined the human psyche using a triplicity of id, ego, and superego.

Beyond the cultural differences between these systems, the characteristics of the three boil down to this:

- The "adult" rational soul

- The "young" or appetite-driven soul

- The wise spiritual or elder soul

In some lines of Feri tradition (including my own), these are called by the friendly titles of Talker, Fetch, and Godself. When I speak of these souls, I might say "the Talker" or "your Talker." That's not unusual. But you might notice that I also sometimes refer to this soul as simply "Talker," the same way you'd call someone by their name. In a way that's what this is, though it's more of a placeholder. I encourage you to name each of your souls to your own liking, once you have a good understanding of them!

Your Talker

Let's begin with your Talker, because they are the easiest to understand of the Three. In our modern culture, we spend most of our time living through this part of us. Talker thinks, plans, reads these words, wrote them. They feel something, and decide what to do about it. It's the job of the Talker to manage numbers and letters and phone calls. They hold the intellect and the more complex emotions, distrust, or disappointment. Both halves of the brain are Talker's domain: the logical, social side and the emotional, personal side. It behooves us all to have these working in concert, to support our ability to think creatively with clarity.

The energy body of Talker is what is commonly called the "aura." It is egg-shaped and extends quite a bit out from the physical form, providing your first contact with the world around you. Your awareness is all around you using this body, and you can receive just as much information from behind as from before. Talker's body tells you when someone's too close or too far away.

THE BODY OF TALKER

Take a minute right now to close your eyes and envision the body of Talker. It may look like a haze of energy of any color in a sort of flattened egg shape. Now envision, with your eyes still closed, what is to either side of you. Now what is above you? And below? And what is behind you? You may find that it's not quite visually that you are perceiving this information, but through some other, less obvious source. This is good. You are opening other ways of "seeing."

Don't worry if this is difficult at first, or if you're not sure whether you're making it all up. Making it up is fine. Exercising the imagination is an important part of this process!

Sometimes Talker gets a bad rap in spiritual communities because it's so close to the "mundane" (as if there were such a thing), but when they are not active or when they are diminished in some way, one quickly loses the capacity to function as a whole person. Is this a bad thing? Most of us would probably say that yes, it is bad! No one wants to forget how to read or call a friend or remember who we are. Mundanity notwithstanding, these are important abilities for a happy life!

But consider this case: a friend's mother had severe dementia just before her death; her Talker had dwindled away. Often, she just wanted to hold hands and watch TV. It took away her judgmental side and her cynicism and allowed her to simply be a creature seeking comfort. So, even though she didn't always recognize my friend as her son, there was a different kind of intimacy to their connection.

Talker's relationship to Fetch is like that of a parent to a child. Talker has the capacity to reason, which Fetch lacks, and Talker can look at a problem, internal or external, and use that beautiful brain to sort out what is needed. Once the reasoning's done, Talker can engage Fetch in a solution.

The relationship between Talker and Godself is a little more difficult. Talker likes to categorize, while Godself sees oneness. Talker is worried we're late, while Godself knows that time is just one convenient way to keep events apart. Fetch can often bridge this gap, taking direction from Godself and prompting a hunch for Talker, or hearing from Talker and sending images and sense-feelings to Godself.

The Talker's job in the secret country expedition is to manage the itinerary, take good notes, and sort out what to do about what is found. Talker is the brains of the operation.

TALKER THOUGHTS
Take a minute now to make a few notes on what you think about the idea of the Talker.
And let's move on.

Your Fetch

Fetch is the Homo sapiens animal self in all its glory, as beautiful and wild as a tiger slinking through the jungle. Think of the human creature without intellect and higher wisdom. That is Fetch.

The primary functions of the Fetch are to be a template for your perfect physical health, to manage energy, to hold your memories, and to communicate easily with Godself.

The energy body of Fetch interpenetrates and extends just a bit beyond the limits of the physical body and might be seen as a red or blue color. It is this interpenetration that allows the Fetch to shift conditions in the physical body.

Fetch is simple in their needs and desires; they speak in pleasure and hunger and pain. Fetch delights in the sensual and gives you that gut feeling that something (or someone) is just dandy, or not quite right.

However, it's important to be careful about how you read these signals.

Fetch will react based on old information if they're not given new information. For instance, if, at some point in your life, you had a traumatic experience with a person who happened to be tall and fair, you may continue to have bad reactions to that physical type unless you actively work to change it. This is going to be a big part of your work with Fetch: getting to know the patterns that are shaping current reactions and then coaxing Fetch to give up those old ideas. Once you become aware of your automatic responses, you can resolve the underlying issues, then relax that control once the healing has taken root. If you move into all your complexes in this way, you eventually find yourself able to trust those instinctive responses. We'll talk more about this when we get to the Shadow House.

Fetch is sometimes referred to as "younger self" because of their simplicity, love of comfort, and lack of filters. It's important to note that this is different from what's commonly called the "inner child." The inner child is a powerful psychological tool for working with that part of you that may have been damaged in your youth, and there is some overlap. However, Fetch is more beast than child (and, of course, sometimes children are very much like beasts, so there is a similarity!). Fetch can be termed "younger" primarily because it resonates on a simple level: every time is now and everything they are experiencing is real, shared or not. Fetch might choose to be uncooperative, but their acting out is more like a dog that's been beat and only remembers how to bite or to hide. They live entirely in the memory that they're experiencing, triggered by whatever event is happening now.

Also, your Fetch is not equipped to lie. They aren't complicated enough to think in terms of truth and untruth.

But this is all too wordy! Try this instead…

THE BODY OF FETCH

Wherever you are at this moment, allow your physical body to relax. Bring into your mind an image of any creature at rest. Perhaps you have a cat or dog at home you've seen in this state and thought, "Dang, that critter has got it easy!" Well, now's your time to come fully into the animal you are and allow your own body to find its most perfectly lazy posture. Just take a few minutes with this and deeply feel your beastly self unfurling inside of you. Yawn, stretch, shift position until you are entirely comfortable. Now practice this whenever you can!

The way to get your Fetch's attention is with pretty smells, yummy foods, rhythmic drumming, chanting/singing, dancing. This is also how you enlist their help in spellcraft or prayer. Fetch takes in the excitement of these things, and you can imagine them jumping up and down with enthusiasm!

It is the gift of Fetch to be able to communicate easily and clearly with the Godself. Their shared language is sensual and symbolic, and there is a natural flow of ideas between them, without all those pesky high-minded words getting in the way.

The task of Fetch in the secret country journey is to sense the surroundings, to move easily between worlds, and to connect with other animal-spirits.

FEELING FETCH

Take a minute here to feel how this idea lands in you. Are you comfortable with yourself as an animal? Why or why not?

Your Godself

Your Godself is the part of you that is in constant connection with all other consciousness, as a molecule in the body of God (or Source, or the Cosmos, or however you prefer to define the "All"). Godself is the soul that vibrates on the highest frequency. Godself holds the vision of the greatest possibilities for your life. They are the model for the best you can be. This is God, no doubt, and it is also you, as an individual. Your Godself is the part that understands what your potential is in this lifetime. They remember what came before this mortal life and will nudge you in the direction of those experiences that support your best growth.

You might say that Godself has the longest view, meaning they can see beyond the mortal perspective. And they don't judge. Their great objectivity points toward the greater good in the long term. Trickily, your Godself's vision of the greater good may be different from yours! Sometimes it's hard to see how challenges and difficulties fit into the overall arc of your life, but you can learn to trust it.

The energy body of Godself is just above your head and may appear as a ball of light or a flower or something else entirely. I like using the image of a crown, which symbolizes my sovereignty over my life.

THE BODY OF GODSELF

Let's see how your Godself appears to you in this moment.

Take a breath. Let the breath you take in fill you and feed you.

Now turn your attention to a spot right above your head and first envision a ball of cobalt blue light. See it a little bigger than a basketball.

See the light gently glowing.

Take three deep breaths with that vision.

Now let the image shift to that of a flower, maybe the same color, maybe different.

This may be a rose or a daisy or dandelion. Just take a moment to see how that looks and feels.

Another three breaths and now let the image shift again to that of a crown, something that a queen or king or quing would wear.

Three breaths more and let it become whatever it becomes.

Breathe into that vision and let it settle in you.

Know that you are one singularly precious being and you are needed.

Try this exercise anytime you are feeling disempowered.

———————

Godself can also change physical reality. When you work magick, this is the part of you that will transform your world (or you), if your connection is strong and your Three Souls are connected in a single purpose.

When you want to pray for or offer good thoughts to another, you can ask that your Godself send to their Godself. Then those two may decide on the best course of action. If you have things you need to tell to someone you can't contact, you can have your Godself speak to them. There is a great family of Godselves, and communication in that realm is instantaneous. We'll practice some of that in the Sanctuary.

Godself is very much at home in the secret country, as they are at home any- and everywhere (and when!). As the part of you that is always connected to all other souls, Godself can arrange meetings, keep you safe, and help you interpret your experiences.

GODSELF'S GIFTS

Think back to the appearance of your Godself. Which one feels most like a benediction? The ball of light? The flower? The crown? Are there any that feel uncomfortable, for whatever reason?

Your Souls Aligned

Now, it's important to keep all these parts of yourself moving in the same direction. The difference between alignment and out-of-alignment is dramatic. For instance, playing music is a physical act that is possible because of the mind's propensity for recognizing patterns. But if you only include Fetch and Talker, it might be said that your playing is technically proficient but lacking in spirit. When you allow Godself to participate, your music becomes transcendent.

Just so, cooking a meal involves shopping, reading, and measuring, in addition to feeling, smelling, and tasting. But when you bring in awareness of the cycles of life and death that support your existence on Earth, you are nourished on a much deeper level.

As you move into the secret country, try to remain attuned to God-self, supportive of Fetch, aware of Talker. The goal is to be in alignment as much as possible. Having your souls in harmony allows you to easily move between the worlds and engage fully wherever you are!

Life-Force, the Ha Prayer, and the Rite of Untangling

Many spiritual systems have a belief in a vital power that is required for body and soul health. What is this power? It's energy, vitality; in Hindu tradition, it is *prana*; in Chinese medicine, it is *qi*; in Huna, it's called *mana*. I usually just call it *life-force*. It is that which enlivens everything, the vital power of all beings.

Throughout these adventures, it's important to remember that you are made of energy. You move through worlds made of energy, worlds you create. By shifting and shaping what you think and see, you can make manifest entirely new experiences.

Spiritual energy is all around us; it is present in all things, including inanimate objects. I would argue that all these have consciousness in some form, from the molecular level on up (and down), and these consciousnesses generate energy. We are literally in a constant energetic conversation with the world around us, giving off heat, taking in fuel—listening and speaking through the movement of this invisible force. Just as matter is not created or destroyed, we do not make life-force, but we do harness it.

What does life-force feel like? How do you recognize it?

The physical body can help you understand this. Think of a blush rising to your cheeks when you are embarrassed. Or the throb of sexual arousal. Or the excitement of a new idea. A rush of life-force can feel like any of those. It can also be a tingling, contraction or expansion, a firming or melting sensation. It usually feels good, though it might be quite intense.

Sometimes you may find yourself experiencing an overabundance of life-force. This might be face-flushing, heart-racing, sweating, hot flashes, feelings of fear and anxiety. There are a few things you can do about this. First, you can send the excess energy up to Godself by blowing great slow breaths in their direction. If you are still feeling unwell, you may lie on the ground and release it into the Earth. This overflow might look like water pooling around you and sinking down into the dirt. This is a gift to the soil, but you will probably be tired after this happens. Eat some food, drink some water, and rest up for next time!

When you are hungry for spiritual energy, you are lethargic, melancholy; you feel depressed and powerless. Ways to build yourself back up include eating healthy food, drumming, chanting, taking a walk, talking to someone you love. I favor listening to good dance music!

Remember that your energy is supposed to rise and fall; everything does. So don't force it. If you exhaust yourself by constantly "rising" at full speed, your "falling" will most likely be dramatic and unpleasant.

Now, let's get to the Ha Prayer.

This prayer works by relying on Fetch's ability to bring in and hold energy. You raise up life-force through a specific breathing technique and let it build until you are full. Then you ask Fetch to keep what they need and blow the rest up to your Godself, just above your head.

The Ha Prayer can be used in many different ways, so state your purpose first. In this case, you're going to be aligning your souls so that they are centered in you and working in harmony.

The Ha Prayer for Triple-Soul Alignment

First, say: May my Three Souls be aligned within me and fully present in this moment.

Breathe deeply. Move into that space inside you that is still and quiet.

Become aware of your Fetch, that part of you that breathes and sleeps and eats and seeks sensual pleasure. The amazing animal Homo sapiens that you are lifts your head to sniff the air, turns your ears toward intriguing sounds, and pushes the juice through you that makes you grow strong and powerful.

This is your deep Self, your animal Soul.

Take a few breaths into that body now, feel the blood flow through your veins, and listen to your faithful heartbeat.

Now take your awareness from that physical space and let it move into the mind space, the thinking and talking space. There is a part of you that plans and decides and reviews and acts; also, it communicates and loves on a higher level than that animal soul.

This part of you is so important, for it lets you share space with your community, with maturity and thoughtfulness and respect.

Take a few breaths into your mind now, see any haze dissipating, know clarity.

Now bring your consciousness to a spot right above your head, where your halo would be if you were an angel (oh wait, you are an angel!). In this sweet spot, there is a part of God that is a part of you that is a part of God. See this as a glowing ball of blue light, shining brilliantly.

This is the part of you that is always in touch with all other beings throughout time and space. This is the part of you that lives in that place of knowing, of oneness.

Take a few breaths into your spirit now, watch the glow become brighter, and feel your connection to all.

Now take one breath and let it filter through and invigorate your physical form, your animal self.

Take another breath and let it move through and awaken your elegant mind, your talking self.

And take another breath and let it brighten and enliven that blue light above you, your divine self.

And another breath, through all three.

When you exhale, blow this energy up to Godself with a long exhalation, or a kiss, or a HA.

Now be still a moment and let Godself's blessing rain down upon you.

———————

Check in with yourself. How do you feel? Different than before? Warm or cool? Tired or wide awake? Maybe you felt nothing to speak of. That's fine. Sometimes it takes a while to get used to the technique and relaxed enough to let the energy flow easily. And you'll have plenty of time to practice because you'll be doing lots of Ha Prayers in different ways as you proceed through your journey!

To keep your souls and thus your life functioning well, it is important to be as free as you can of complexes created by self-doubt, misplaced anger, and fear.

Being clear in this way can be your best protection in any situation. If you are shiny, insults are reflected off you. If you have no insecurities for it to stick to, disrespect slides away. When you are full of confidence in yourself, there is no room for others' judgments!

A common and simple way of working toward this state of clarity is the Untangling Rite or the "Rite of Unbinding." A basic principle of this rite is that your life-force belongs to you and you get to decide how to use it. You don't necessarily want to cut away your problems; this would rid you of some of your energy. Instead you can find the places where you are all tangled up about the circumstances of your situation and free yourself from those complications. Sometimes this means that things do go away, but other times it just means that you find new ways of seeing people and problems and become more easeful in dealing with them.

In this rite, water is used as a sacred holder of your complexes for a time while you heal them. Its nature is softening and separating, which helps to loosen the tangles and knots. You might choose to have a special cup that is only used for this.

In the same way that a Buddhist teacher might tell you, if you have a problem, to "take it to the meditation cushion," we sometimes say, "put it in the cup!"

The ritual of untangling is important, but it is only one tool. Having the rite be the only time you focus on your spiritual health is sort of like sinning all week and then going to church on Sunday to be forgiven. It's not a really good program for creating joyful, empowered beings. It's better to be aware of your actions and your motivations every day. Check in with yourself and with trusted others: Is this the good kind or the bad kind of selfish? Is this fear to be listened to or overcome?

It's important to get okay with seeing your foibles, what you might think of as your "defects," not because it's pleasant in any way, but because it's a necessary step in the process. I was lucky enough to receive this advice from a good friend: just because you admit you're being a jerk doesn't mean you get to continue to be one, but knowing that it's happening is the first step to changing your behavior!

You can take inventory, and consider how you treat yourself and others. You can make new choices about how you want to proceed. And please, never forget to be gentle with yourself.

The Untangling Rite
Thank the cup for partaking in this rite with you.

Pour clear water in.

Take a small sip and thank the water for helping you with this work.

Set the cup down.

Cup your hands and make an energetic container there, like a sphere or an egg.

Breathe four breaths into your hands, sending forth those things within you that need tending, those things that have forgotten their true nature of joy and creativity.

Hold these things in your hands for a moment, then place them into the cup, into the sacred water, which is all water, a source of healing and transformation.

Hold your hands to either side, or above and below the cup.

Begin to breathe life-force as for a Ha Prayer.

Send the life-force into the cup, letting it flow through your hands, letting it bless and purify the water, soothing and smoothing all you've placed in it.

Breathe out all the air you have in you, then let your body breathe in.

Hold this breath in, and then drink all the water.

Welcome back into you this, your own life-force, which has been cleansed and charged with your blessing.

Hold yourself and feel the energy move through you, back to its rightful place, as strong and healthy as possible for today.

Blessed be.

———————

Take a moment to simply attend to yourself. Where is your mind? How is your body? What about your heart?

Values and Virtues

Now, I must inform you that there is a downside to all this lovely cleansing and aligning work. The discrepancies between how you think you are (or would like to be) and how you really are, day to day, are going to show up with a vengeance. You may have thought of yourself as a basically kind-hearted person, but your self-reflection may show that you are actually sort of selfish. Or you may see yourself as fair-minded until you find yourself crossing the street when a certain kind of person comes toward you.

And that's okay.

The revelation of your imperfection, I mean. Not the meanness and the racism.

It's been said that our ability to see our foibles comes before our ability to fix them, which can be really discouraging when we're starting a new spiritual practice. When I started doing daily prayers to "know myself," I thought, dang! Daily prayers have made me more mean! But, guess what. I'd always been like that; I just hadn't seen it before.

I was mightily disturbed, and you may be, too.

There is a way to manage this issue. You can get better at living in accordance with what you believe. Clarifying your values will give you a guiding star (or constellation, more like) for your behavior.

If you don't choose your own ideals, the world will happily impose on you. According to the popular media, you should make lots of money (greed); get them before they get you (paranoia); want something for nothing (selfishness); worship convenience (thoughtlessness); feel terrorized (fear); hate belly fat (shame); and fix those wrinkles (vanity). Not a nice list, is it?

To move toward your spiritual development, you have to be willing to stand firm in pursuit of what you think is right. The creation of a free, just, and pleasurable society requires powerful people with integrity to act in support of freedom and justice and pleasure.

In the secret country, I ask you to hold an attitude of creativity and compassion, with an undercurrent of joy; I would also like you to use your powers of discernment freely. I might call these the virtues ("values given moral weight") of this system. And it's important to act in support of your virtues. "Faith without works is dead," sayeth the Christian Bible and a lot of other folks. What I've done today to live according to my virtues is to work on this book, have some big laughs with my husband, speak kindly, and try to stay out of love with my own opinions.

The core of it is simply this: How are you making the world more like you want it to be? What are you doing to form your life into a strong, fun place to live? In *Batman Begins*, Rachel says to Bruce Wayne (after seeing him act like an entitled jerk), "It's not who you are underneath, it's what you do that defines you." I believe that wholeheartedly.

While we're traveling together, I will assume that you are willing to work with the values of the secret country along with your own, if they are different. You could just adopt these values long term, or those of some other system that appeals to you. Some people come to their values because of their class or profession: Bushido, the code of conduct for samurai in Japan, lists seven virtues. The chivalric code of the medieval knights is similar, not surprising for warriors. On the other hand, doctors hold to the Hippocratic oath to "First, do no harm."

Or you might follow the virtues of your chosen faith: The Christian Bible offers the Ten Commandments; the Koran offers a similar list of admonitions; Buddhism offers the Four Noble Truths; and in Pagan circles, we find the Nine Noble Virtues of Heathenry, the Eightfold Path of Wicca, or the Iron and Pearl Pentacles of Feri tradition. For the atheists, Alain de Botton has described ten virtues for the modern age.

These are all well and good, but I'd like to suggest that you take some time to figure out your own, aside from or in addition to what your religion (or lack thereof) teaches.

Making Your Core Values Pentacle

For the purposes of this exercise, you are going to organize your thoughts using a pentacle. There is a good reason for this, other than because I'm Witchy and I like pentacles. To choose two of anything means that those two things hold equal approximate weight. Make it three and it becomes just a bit more complex. If it's four, then you're always looking at two and two. But oh, delightful five! That extra one invigorates the thought process and gives so many wonderful connections to explore between the points. Also, the pentacle gives you a pattern that will map to your physical body so you can move the energy of your values through and around you. More on that later!

First, take a look at the list of values in appendix A. Go through and put a star next to all the words that immediately attract your attention. Go back through and begin to cull, or sort. You may create a separate group of five for your work life, for your love life, for your spiritual life, and so on, but when you are finished, you should have one pentacle (to rule them all!) that encompasses the primary virtues that you choose to live by.

Don't get ensnared by the it-has-to-be-right monster. You have as many chances as you want. In fact, it is a good thing to go back and review and revise your pentacles periodically, to make sure they still work for you. If you have chosen to make multiple pentacles, you will almost certainly have changes to make, especially when your life circumstances change.

Now, draw a pentacle. Or print one off the Internet, which is actually much easier! Write your five values on sticky notes and place them on the points of the pentacle. Think about the relationships between them. You can see how there will be two "legs" to each point, which end in two other points. Do those two support the one? Does any particular one come first? Or last? Remember, in a circle (the "-cle" of the "penta-cle"), there is not necessarily a firm beginning or end; it can go 'round and 'round and 'round. Move the words from place to place until they feel right.

Once you've made your pentacle, see how well it lines up with your actual life. Think about each point in detail. If "thrift" is a value for you, would you have bought that new phone? Maybe that purchase does support your thriftiness because you got a great new data plan with it, or maybe you just really wanted it!

See if you are truly living in support of your values, and if you are not, ask yourself why. Is it because you just wish this was a value for you, when it really isn't? Or is it because you are afraid to live closer to your truth? You will find places where you are out of touch with what is important to you. Would you like to line up your life? Maybe you always considered your family to be top priority, but you find that you are spending all your time at work. Does that line up? Maybe it does if your kids are older and no longer need (or want!) your participation in everything they do.

Or maybe it doesn't if your boss is making unreasonable demands. How would you like to deal with that?

Maybe you'll choose to acknowledge the truths you've revealed and run with them. At one point in my wildly variant career, I was designing commercial interiors. My clients were people who had a lot of money, just the kind of people I had always thought (without knowing any) were greedy and selfish. At my job, I was learning that simply having big bucks doesn't make someone a bad person, but I was struggling with my old hippie-chick idealism. Finally, my husband said to me, "Do you think you're betraying your ideals by enjoying working with these people?" and I broke down, because it was true. And I had to realize that I wasn't betraying anything. I was just updating my values to acknowledge my new experience of money, which upon reflection encouraged me to further commit to supporting the causes I felt strongly about. With money I made from working with people who had money.

Do you need to shift your perception? Or your activities? Are there actions that you can take right now that will move you closer to your ideals? Take your time with your deliberations.

When you've got a good idea of what your final pentacle configuration will be, try this:

Running Your Values Pentacle

Stand with feet apart and arms outstretched.

Imagine that your pentacle is superimposed on your body, with your head at the top and the lower left point at your right foot. Do the points fit where they fall? Do you need to rearrange them so they are in a better order?

Say the name of the point at your head and see a glow there. What is the shape of it? The size? Does it appear healthy? Spend a moment here, just observing. Now allow your attention to fall to your right foot. Say the name of the point there and again observe the shape, color, and size of it. Take a deep breath. Bring your attention up to your left hand. Say the name of the point there. See it in all its strength or weakness. Breathe into it. Now to your right hand. Name the point. Observe. No judgment. Breathe. Now to your left foot. Name it. See it. Again, deep breath.

Now you have five glowing points around you, each named as one of your primary values. Notice whether any of them appear diminished, if the colors are different. Are you drawn to bring breath and energy to any of them?

To balance the points, run your attention through the pentacle again: head, right foot, left hand, right hand, left foot, and back to your head. Let this go on for as long as you like. Two or three minutes is a good start.

Now you have claimed what is important to you. There is another step to ensure that you are centered in your own values. Send your awareness around the circle the points make: head, left hand, left foot, right foot, right hand, head, and so on. Recognize that all that is within this circle of glowing light is you—your fears and your joys, all that makes you who you are. Outside this boundary is not-you, and while it may trouble you, it might not be your problem to fix.

Hearken back to your experience in the Soul-Fire Invocation. Remember how it felt to be completely filled with your own selfhood, alive and alight with your singular power. Let that feeling empower this circle and let it become a shield made of your commitment to serve your values.

When you are ready, allow the energy to soften back into you. Pat your body all over. Have a snack.

Living in accordance with your own values makes you strong, flexible, and confident. Your spiritual work builds power, and it's good to be conscientious about how you use that power. Every decision we make has repercussions.

Keep in mind that when a seed begins to grow, the first thing it does is break the case that holds it. Sometimes things get broken when you take action. Often, it's worth it. It's up to you to decide when that is true.

Unpacking the Values Pentacle

Take a few minutes to write about how it feels to run this energy through you. There is big magick in the places between the points. How do they relate to each other? Are there ways that strengthening one can support them all?

Morning Practice

A morning practice is helpful for staying in touch with your intention for your life, being attuned to your priorities, and staying clean in your relationships. Make this part of your routine. Even a few times a week is helpful.

- Soul-Fire Invocation

- Ha Prayer

- Untangling Rite

- Running Your Values Pentacle

——— *Three* ———

GATHERING
THE GEAR

It's time for a break. You join the rest of the students in the small kitchen. Strangely, the table is bigger than you first thought; there is space for everyone to sit and enjoy a cup of coffee or tea. The room is warm and smells deliciously like fresh-baked bread. On the board are several loaves just out of the oven and thick slabs of butter and homemade jams. The peaches you noticed earlier are being cut up to share, along with apples and berries that you suspect were grown right here. The food and the company are delightful. In a short while, it is time to get back to work. You return to the larger room with the great windows.

———

Now you have some tools and techniques to build power and stay clear; you've done the difficult work of examining your personal values and integrity. Your morning practice is happening. The next step is to begin building a bridge between the shared reality and the secret country. You'll do this by creating a special altar that will become your anchor in both places.

Your Home Base

Remember, this is all about making your adventures wildly magickal, deeply intense, totally fun, and extremely safe. By purposefully making connections between realities, you allow this safe, fun, intense magick to permeate all the worlds you travel in. Some of the items you'll be gathering for your home base will have a counterpart in the secret country that you might become allies with. Some of these are traditional items used in neo-pagan Witchcraft, which you may already have and have magickal purposes for. Other items are specifically to be used to record your experiences and make the map of the places you visit. (That's my favorite part!)

The gathering of materials is an opportunity to express who you are and how you want to be. This includes what you wear on your travels, where you keep your altar, what's on it, what music you listen to, and so on. The style of sketchbook or notebook you use and what you use to write, draw, and color in it are up to you.

As much as possible, you will want to create a setting in the physical realm that supports your work in the secret country. If you can make a permanent place for these outings (innings?), so much the better. In the best-case scenario, everyone would have a big, secluded space to themselves, quiet and well-lit, with a comfy chair and a door that locks. Alas, most of us don't have a setup quite that fancy, so if your space is humbler than that, it'll be fine. As long as you can create a little bit of privacy for yourself, you'll be good.

Now, let's start with the altar. Some of you may already have many altars. If you do, that's great. You can add your secret country gear to it, or create a new one, if you like.

Maybe you don't have an altar; maybe you even feel like you don't know how to make one. I beg to differ. I've met very few people who don't have at least one altar in their home or workplace, though they might not think of it that way. Take a look around your house. Do you have a spot for family pictures? Shells you found at the beach? Your diploma? Is there a mantel above your fireplace with holiday decorations? Maybe a hand-made piece of art from a dear friend?

All of these might be considered altars for various purposes: honoring kin, extolling your accomplishments, attuning to the season. I might consider my desk as an altar to my writing. Or my kitchen counter as an altar to my family's well-being and nutrition. If you think about it in this way, it becomes a less intimidating concept. An altar is simply a workspace devoted to a particular kind of work, something that is important enough that it deserves its own dedicated area.

Now, the secret country altar doesn't need to be fancy, unless you want it to be. I'm a Dirt-Witch, so I like things simple, but you might love intricacy. I have an old white cotton curtain on my altar, but you might want embroidered silk. *To each their own* is the motto of this work! The main consideration is that there is space for the tools and materials you will need, and those are quite simple.

The Secret Country Starter Kit

- **A cup**

  A cup is a symbol of receptivity and also hospitality! At any given moment, you are ready to raise a glass with those you meet. It's convivial. The style of cup doesn't matter. If you can drink out of it, it will do. This may be the same as your untangling cup, or something different.

- **A good pen**

  You will keep notes on your travels, so make sure you have a writing implement handy. It's no fun to go searching for something to write with when you are trying to maintain a meditative state.

- **A not-really-nice notebook**

  A journal is helpful for immediately recording your experiences, but often your words right after meditation will be rambling and strange. That is awesome! Your mind is free! But you may feel pressure to keep a nice book nice, so use a cheap notebook or sketchbook. Something unlined will allow your writing to wander at will and give you room for drawings and diagrams.

- **A really nice notebook**

  You'll be creating an important magickal tool as you venture through these landscapes: a travelogue for the secret country of yourself. This fancier book will stand ready to hold your edited writings and more carefully crafted diagrams and drawings of your destinations.

- **A piece of poster board, foam core, or plain cardboard**

  This will be the proto-map of the secret country of yourself. I call it "proto-" because I don't want you to be intimidated by it. It will be messy. It should be! And it is going to change, probably a lot, over time. Use sticky notes at first. Then add more elaborate images as it seems appropriate. Also, feel free to make an entirely new map whenever it's needed. My point is, don't start with the fanciest stuff. You will surely be making changes.

- **A recording device**

  It is good to record the meditations for yourself if you aren't working with a group. The best way to do this is to speak clearly and very slowly. It's difficult to speak *too* slowly in a meditation. As noted, leave time for exploration in each location you visit, then record the last part, which is designed to bring you safely out of your trance state. If you are going to use a cell phone to make your recordings, keep it on airplane mode. Otherwise, the distractions can be too tempting!

Making the Altar

Not all these items need to fit on top of whatever you choose for your altar. Sometimes there's an overflow, which is okay, because really the whole area around an altar can be considered sacred. So, you might keep your notebooks underneath it or the poster board behind it.

In fact, your altar might only hold a cup, a pen, and a recording device at first. This leaves lots of space for your personal items. For instance, you might want to have at hand some of the other traditional tools of Witchcraft. You already have the cup, but how about a knife, plate, and candle? These four are representative of the elements of air, water, earth, and fire, whose realms you'll visit later.

There are other objects common to many spiritual practices: incense for cleansing the air or bringing in particular energies, water for cleansing and cooling, salt to taste to bring you back into your body. You might include offerings of food and drink, flowers, or other plants that you tend for those spirits you work with in the secret country. Stones and crystals are also popular and become even more potent when you engage them on the deeper level of the inner realms.

Also, you might like to include shells, pinecones, or other natural objects. These are excellent ways to stay in touch with the energies of a place you've visited, but do be sensitive about what you collect. Nature is using every bit of her parts for something, and it's easy to cause unintended consequences.

Depending on your personal leanings, you might keep images of your gods, your ancestors, or other spirits on your altar. For some folks, celebrities or historical figures serve as demigods. I might date myself here, but currently I'm fond of the actress Angelina Jolie as an avatar of courageous compassion because of her diplomatic work with the United Nations. In another realm, Susan B. Anthony might inspire you because of her influence on the women's suffrage movement. You could even work with superheroes or other fantasy personalities to inspire you. How about Wonder Woman for strength, intelligence, courage, and beauty? Or Gandalf the wizard for wisdom, magickal skill, and power? The point is that if you are connected to and inspired by anyone (or anything), honor your inner knowing and let it be a part of your practice.

What else belongs in your sacred space? How about images of beautiful, faraway (or nearby) places? Books of poetry? Inspirational art? Or beloved pieces of music? Include whatever feels important to you.

And remember: each of these things has their own spirit. Books and music and shells each have their own spirit, active in the secret country.

The setting around the altar is important, too. Fetch should be comfortable, so a warm, soft space is good. It really is best to have a door you can lock, if possible, to help Fetch feel safe. Godself will feel welcome in an environment of calm and quiet. Talker has their own needs as well, so make sure your pens have ink and you have a thesaurus available in case of a poetry emergency!

Keep in mind that when you return from each of your meditations, you will need some time and space to relax, to integrate your experiences and work on your creative expression. So, don't schedule yourself too tightly. Depending on what's happened in your journey, you might want an hour or even more.

One thing that sometimes happens during a meditation is that you'll fall dead asleep. Some folks find that troubling. I'm here to tell you: don't worry about it! Sometimes your adventures will uncover issues that are particularly difficult to manage, and Fetch decides that "checking-out" is the best course of action. The process continues. If you are strongly concerned about this possibility, try standing up for the meditation or sitting in a less than perfectly comfortable chair. You might also like to set an alarm for an hour after you begin or add some sort of tone to wake you at the end of the recording you make.

And do make sure to eat a little something and drink some water when you return from your journeys. Spending time in the spiritual (or imaginative) territories can leave you a little off-kilter. Eating something hearty and making sure you are hydrated are good ways to remind yourself that you are a human creature and that the shared reality is your home.

Take some time to plan out your workspace. Are there items you want to bring to your altar? Are there tools you would like to acquire? Go ahead and start gathering your materials and making a good space for them.

Recording for Posterity (Or Just for Yourself)

There are many ways to bring your secret country adventures into the shared reality. You may craft, write, and pray a bridge between the worlds. The outward expression of your inner experience allows you to inhabit those places more deeply and create lasting memories from what you find. Inviting your Talker, Fetch, and Godself to participate in this process anchors it throughout your being.

Your Three Souls are different from each other, and they are enchanted by different things. With Fetch, it's simple: good smells, pretty colors, body movement. Talker is more complex: puzzles, prose, information. Godself speaks through the noble virtues: truth, grace, love. To engage them in your creative expression means to take into account what they are good at and provide a path for them to work their own ways through the secret country. Like how, you say? Like this:

Crafting about your experience is good. Fetch likes to make things. Manifestation is their stock in trade. Hold gently in your mind's eye the place you have been as you apply pencil to paper, paint to canvas, or hands to clay. Perhaps your method of operation is more along the lines of improvisational dance, or yoga. Maybe you move things through you by ripping up old photos or love letters and burning them. You should have some sort of tangible result when you're done: a sketch, painting, or sculpture; a sweaty and sore body; a pile of ashes. Happy Fetch!

Thinking and learning about what you find is good. Some of us are a little too adept at this, though! When anything new arises we automatically hit the Internet for all the info we can get. We sort and bookmark and label and print. But this is not expression; it's the opposite. We are filling ourselves with someone else's words and thoughts. It's important to have information (impression). And it's more important to this process that you use Talker tools to put your thoughts where you can see them (expression). So, gather the information and then make a plan. Write it out. Use that intricate mind of yours to record your truth. Do you need to see a healer about this? Do you need to do a ritual about it? Write about how you think this is affecting you and how you might be changed by dealing with it.

Praying about your adventures is good. Remember, Godself is the part of you that is a part of God that is a part of you, and so on. Praying to your own Godself is perfectly appropriate. Where the results of your engagement with Fetch and Talker can be seen, the expressions of Godself are usually felt. A lightness in the chest, a rise of warmth flowing through you, a feeling of being in exactly the right place at exactly the right time (even if you're waiting for the bus in the rain!) are all ways that Godself speaks through you. It's trickier to purposefully seek to open Godself's ability to act in the worlds. It involves quieting down and letting things flow; you are listening for the still, small voice within you. Things you can do to make yourself more adept at this are walking in nature, listening to inspiring music (David Bowie, anyone?), looking at art, being in awe.

Of course, all your parts are involved in all that you do, but some activities are more clearly aligned with one or the other.

Most important to this process of expression is this: *you proceed with or without confidence.* You move forward not knowing if what you do is "good." It doesn't matter. Do not let discomfort stop you! At some point you may choose to have the discipline and do the hard work that's needed to become excellent at one of these skills, but for now, let the critic be quiet. You should feel free to fail (also known as "learning").

There's a strange thing that happens with humans. If we actually feel fear about a thing, it feels important and like a worthy adversary. We will challenge that brute and get past it! But more often it's a milder form of anxiety that defeats us: awkwardness. We're not sure what to do, or we think we'll look stupid or that others will judge us. All those things may be true. But stepping into action in that case is big magick. Awkwardness signifies an opportunity for real change.

Throughout our time together, you will be asked to practice expressing what is happening for you, through the lenses of Talker, Godself, and Fetch. These practices fall under the categories of head, heart, and hands. It works best if you take time soon after your trance work to do the activities so your visions don't get lost in your return to the shared reality.

At the beginning of any of these activities, take five minutes to sit in silence, become aware of your breath, and remember what you are doing. Nothing you create or experience needs to make sense to anyone else. Or even to yourself. Don't use your intention as a stick to beat your expression into a certain shape.

For any of the head, heart, hands sections, substitute any other activity from these lists and modify as desired.

Forms of Creative Expression		
Talker: Head	Godself: Heart	Fetch: Hands
playing an instrument	trance-journeying	jewelry making
spell crafting	divination	drumming
writing words	looking at art	collaging
guided trance-work	dreaming	cooking

Forms of Creative Expression		
Talker: Head	Godself: Heart	Fetch: Hands
writing music	meditating	painting
research	listening to music	sculpting
planning	walking in nature	yoga
graphing	free (or automatic) writing	sketching
life time-line	praying	crafting (making things)
making puzzles	reading poetry	dancing
organizing	going to church	singing

Your Travelogue and Map

Collaging: Art for Everyone!

Collaging is probably the easiest form of capturing the images of the places you visit in the secret country. With a pile of *National Geographic*, *Smithsonian*, *Architectural Digest*, and even fashion magazines, you are sure to find images that speak to your experiences.

HERE'S WHAT YOU NEED:

Magazines, or other source of images (you can
    even google pictures for your specific needs)

Double-sided tape or glue stick

Scissors

Poster board or foam core (or just any old piece of cardboard)

Any other decorative things, like glitter or ribbon or paper
    cutouts or anything else that can be glued or taped in place

HERE'S HOW YOU DO IT:

Holding in mind the image of where you've been, begin flipping pages of the magazines. Be careful you don't get stuck reading articles. Talker is insatiably curious and will derail this process if allowed to.

Tear out pictures without worrying too much about how they will fit or even what they mean. This is a Fetch-oriented deal, so it doesn't need to make sense to your brain.

After you have a bunch of images, decide which one goes in the middle. This may be the largest one, or the most important one, if those are not the same.

It is easier to place larger images first, then smaller.

Overlapping is good and gives more complexity to the design.

Cut or tear the edges of the images so that they fit properly. Cutting gives a polished feel, but tearing has its own charm.

Place everything first before gluing or taping anything to make sure you like the overall design.

When you're ready, attach the images. Keep going until you feel done.

This is a work of magick. It can be a form of divination where you are seeking understanding from your deeper aspects. If you finish the collage and there is something not right about it, figure out what needs to be changed, find those other images, and glue them over the original. You may choose to make an entirely new collage instead. But don't forget that this is a process, not only of description, but also of revelation. Meet what is revealed to you with an open mind, listen to it, then change it if necessary.

Travelogue Pages

Throughout your wanderings, there will be time to make notes about the places you'll visit. This is the beginning of the travelogue of your journey.

Your travelogue should remind you of where you went and when, who or what went with you, what you saw and experienced, and how you think and feel about it. You might also include drawings or sketches or even images of the locations. Consider taking a photo of your collage and making that part of the entry.

This is a good way to format those pages in your nice journal so you can transcribe your original notes into a thing of beauty.

- Where did you go?

- On what day? What phase was the moon in? Were there any other interesting astrological factors?

- Who accompanied you? What tools did you bring or use?

- Was it easy to get there, or was it difficult? Did you have any interruptions?

- What did the place look like? How did it sound? Smell? How was the weather?

- Did you meet anyone there? What was that like?

- How do you feel about this place? Are you looking forward to going back? Are there other things you'd want to bring with you when you go?

- Is there anything you need to do in the shared reality to support your experience in the secret country of yourself?

- Do you need to schedule a time to go back to that specific locale?

Making the Map

It's tricky to bring a landscape as ephemeral as the secret country of yourself into the shared reality. But it's interesting and important to see how places connect to each other, what their relationship is, and where they may overlap.

A good way to start the map is with sticky notes and a big piece of paper, poster board, or foam core. Begin by making a set of notes that read: Sanctuary, Shadow House, Temple, School, realm of air, realm of fire, realm of water, realm of earth, heart of the cosmos, heart of the earth. After you've begun your travels, place a note on the map. Your Sanctuary is often in the middle, but it may not be. I've had the experience of finding that my Sanctuary wants to hide out in a corner. When that happens, I want to check in with myself to see if I'm feeling threatened and wanting to have my back protected.

In this way, the map becomes a diagnostic tool as well as a magickal working. I can choose to do more protective practices to see if that helps me to want to move back into the center of my world.

You might consider the map to be a microcosm of your life. See how important education is to you by how close the School is to your Sanctuary. Find the relationship between the Shadow House and the Temple. And even though the realms of the elements are placed at the points of the compass in the meditations, they might show up differently on the map. What's the relationship between the Cemetery and the realm of earth? Or the heart of the cosmos?

If you are artistically inclined, you can get as fancy as you'd like with the map. If you think you are bad at art, then don't think of this as art! It's simply a way of keeping track of where you are. Do what works for you.

The map is also a good way to feel out where your other places are. In this particular journey I'm taking you on, we will visit certain locales, but your secret country is infinite and unlike anyone else's. You should absolutely show on the map the places that only exist for you: the river of forgiveness, the oasis of your marriage, the playground at the school, or the croquet court at the temple.

And the map will probably change over time. Notice when it starts feeling wonky. Is it taking you longer than usual to get to the School? Do you want that to be different? Take a class in the shared reality. Is your

Temple getting hard to find? Maybe pump up your spiritual practices, whatever they may be.

The secret country of yourself and the shared reality have an effect on each other; they can support each other or drag each other down. So it's a good idea to pay attention to what your internal and external lives are each calling for.

—— Four ——

INVITING ALLIANCES

ime for another break. The woman next to you stands, slowly unbending her knees. She reaches high above her head and you hear the cracking of her joints. She smiles ruefully at you. "Gettin' old," she says. You smile back in sympathy. Wondering if there are any peaches left, you meander into the kitchen. A few others are sitting there, and they smile in greeting. You find one last peach and hold it for a moment, feeling the fuzziness of the skin. After asking if anyone wants to share it (answer: no), you lift it to your nose to breathe in its voluptuous scent and finally take a bite. As your teeth pierce the skin, there's a tiny explosion of juice that runs down your chin. Laughing, someone hands you a napkin. You laugh, too, happy to be among such kind and thoughtful people. Soon it's time to return to the big room to continue your lessons.

Magickal Community

Okay, quick question: Who here has a problem asking for help? Yes, pretty much everyone. That's par for the course. But here's the thing: humans are tribal animals. We are meant to rely on each other for fellowship, healing, comfort, and affection. This does not make us weak. It makes us strong. This is true in the shared reality, as well as every other reality. We need community, in person or online, magickal and otherwise.

So it's time to think about who wants to join you on the journey. Who is ready to (and deserves to) share your joy and excitement and possibly fear? Who knows their way around the liminal spaces between worlds, between neurons, between you and the rest of your life?

Who will be your champion? Your Sherpa? Your guide?

Remember, you are looking for those who can support you in connecting with and aligning your Fetch, *and* Talker, *and* Godself. Not *only* Godself, *or* Talker, *or* Fetch. So you might find yourself lighting candles to call to you the spirits you need, but it also might mean calling your doctor. It might mean finding a therapist, a bodyworker, or an art teacher! Allies from all walks of life are important.

It might be completely clear to you who you want to enlist. If you work with a coven or other magickal working group, it is a great choice to do this journeying together and support each other on your ways. If you have a sympathetic counselor, you should let them know that you're going to be doing some personal exploration. If you're in a solid love relationship, of whatever stripe, consider letting that person in on the plan.

Exploring the secret country is an internal experience, but it will affect the rest of your life. The shift in your energy, intention, and attention will show up at your work-for-money, your work-at-home, your loves and friendships, wherever they occur. Your growth and development affect all the worlds you come in contact with. That's the beauty of our inter-being. So why not bring some of those folks along to begin with?

A few different things happen when you do this work with a group. One is that you foster connection with others. When you allow another person to hear about your inner worlds, there is a real intimacy created. The intimacy can work in a couple of different ways, too. With those you don't know at all, the distance you feel can allow you to speak much more freely about the circumstances of your life in the shared reality. With those who have no vested interest in your problems, you may find their objectivity helps you to get a fresh perspective.

On the other hand, you might find that the secret country work allows you to be present in your existing relationships with new clarity and commitment. Hearing about the intricacies of your partners' inner worlds can give you a greater appreciation for the mystery that lies within them.

Another thing that happens is your vision is expanded. Sometimes it is in someone else's story that your own limits are lifted and you can see greater possibilities. In one of my weekend workshops, an attendee told me that she was hesitant to talk about her secret country because what she was seeing in her meditations was something different from what other people were describing. She spoke specifically about her Library being huge and shimmering with the crystals that were the books. And truly, I had seen many Libraries at that point but never one like that. However, as she described it, the vision became clear to me, and a new door was opened in my own inner world. A huge expansion occurred in that moment, and I realized, again, that in this place, anything is possible.

Another person related to me that when he was trying to find his Sanctuary, he crossed a bridge onto a forested island. He was looking for a building until he got the clear message that what he sought was *there* in that spot—no walls, only trees, and that the bridge was only there for him. (Again, my husband. Again, why I adore him.)

The other thing that happens when you work with a group is you are pushed beyond your normal boundaries and might discover new resources within yourself. If nothing else, the presence of others will evoke responses that are important for you to see. You can learn from every experience, including (or especially) those that are uncomfortable.

In discomfort, you are forced to step out of your usual way of doing and defining things. Most of us would do just about anything to avoid confrontation. But that's where the magick is; friction between people, places, and things provides energy that you can use for positive change.

In a good working group, the participants make a commitment to be honest with one another, but also sensitive. Is your feedback thoughtful? Is it necessary? Is it kind? For your travels to bear fruit, it is crucial to practice compassion for others and for yourself. There is a good chance that you will find troubling things in the secret country. A good ally on this journey will support you and also not let you avoid responsibility for your part in those troubles!

Guides and Guardians

Before beginning this grand tour, you want to know that you have some help on "the other side," apart from the shared reality.

Now it's time to call on those who can help you in this work and play. Though you may meet many guides and guardians and allies during your time in the secret country, there is one who will be with you most often, your personal master teacher, your sensei, your mentor, possibly your partner-in-crime! That's who you call for first. This might be someone you know, a spirit-guide from way back, or it may be someone new. It may be an ancestor of blood or spiritual lineage, or a descendant, or a future self. It might be a wolf or a dog or a tree, or all these at different times. In the secret country, a single personality can show up in many forms!

In his book *God is a Verb*, Rabbi David Cooper talks about how the primary difference between angels and demons is that the angels are leading us toward god and the demons away from god. I take this to mean that the spirits who mean you well or ill may use the exact same methods, but the ends are different. In other words, you can't assume that hurtful experiences are actually harmful in the long run. The biggest challenges will often be brought by those who have the utmost faith in your capability, sometimes far beyond what you think you can handle.

So, if your guide or guardian seems unkind or overly harsh, you might give them a little time before giving them the boot. They may be an angel disguised as a butt-kicking coach!

But, if someone appears as your neglectful mother or your abusive father, you are perfectly within your rights to say, "No, thank you!" (or something stronger) and end the interaction. Then take a step back, breathe, and realign your souls with the stated intention of having God-self take full part in your journey. Then send out the call again with the stronger protection and care of your own divinity.

Also, you might find that it is your own Godself who chooses to walk with you, in their usual form or not. That's perfectly okay, too!

Seeking the Ally

Find a comfortable place. Begin with your Ha Prayer for Triple-Soul Alignment on page 28. This will ensure that you are fully aligned and present before you call for assistance.

Next, let the breath you take in fill you and feed you. Let the breath you take in invigorate the eye of the storm within your physical form, the place of stillness and calm that is always within you. Breathe into that place. With physical eyes closed, open etheric sight. If you are not sure what you see, or if you think you may be making it up, good! That's fine for now.

Take another breath into the center of you and let a light open within you like a beacon, and let a call go out from you, to the one who will be your ally, guide, and guardian.

Creatures of Knowledge and Wisdom,
Beings of Power and Grace, I call to you.
I am young in this craft and seek assistance.
Show me the road to understanding.
Give me courage that I may face my fears.
Help me to see my revelations with clarity.
I offer myself to the path of self-knowledge.

I commit myself to the path of self-healing.

I trust that all is for my highest good in the end.

Bless me and blessed be.

Let that beacon shine for a bit and see who comes to you. Let them take form with you, and spend some time connecting with them. Remember that allies may shift shape, depending on your needs at the time.

If no one appears for you, invite Yoda, Dumbledore, or any other character who strikes you as wise and powerful. Personally, I favor the Bulletproof Monk!

Take at least five minutes with this helping spirit and tell them of your desires and challenges with this work.

Now prepare to move back into the shared reality. Ask your guide how you might find them again, within this space and without.

And when you are ready, come back to the breath. Breathe in, and let the breath you take in invigorate your physical form and remind you of your body, where you sit, and what supports your flesh. Breathe into your body and out, into your body and out, breathe into your body and follow your breath back out into the room of light and noise and shared reality. And when you are ready, open your eyes and be here now.

Take some notes on your experience. Drink water and eat food. Get centered in your flesh.

Now you've reached out for the one who will go with you into the secret country. But there are other allies that are already close at hand: the tools that will accompany you in your explorations. Back in chapter 3, you began putting together an altar. Now you will find a new way to connect to your tools and other items of power.

Talking to Your Tools

The cup you choose could be a mason jar or a crystal goblet. I like things that are hard to break, so I usually use a jar. However, as you get farther into the secret country, you might meet some folks you'd rather honor with something fancier. Royals often like a cup that's a bit more refined.

Make sure your cup is physically clean. For this item, I'm going to suggest only using food-grade cleansers such as salt water or water containing rosemary or lavender oil. Rinse it with clear water and dry it well.

Go to your altar and take your comfortable position there. Notice the shape of your cup, the color. Feel the outside and the inside of the bowl; are there different thicknesses in the material? Use your eyes and your hands to investigate it thoroughly. Again, admire its beauty.

Deep breaths. Close eyes. See the cup, its curves and edges. Imagine its temperament. Tempting seductress? Dreamy poet? Surreal artist? Or something different? Take your time to seek the personality of your cup.

When you have that established, introduce yourself. Explain the Untangling Rite and ask for their help. If you get a negative response, find another cup. If you hear nothing, or if you get a positive response, proceed. Check whether there's anything they want from you. Chat for a bit.

Then it will be time to return to the shared reality. Say goodbye to the spirit of the cup.

Open your eyes and fill the cup with water. Drink it down, feeling the pressure of your lips on the cup. Let your drinking be like a kiss (if you and the cup are both amenable!).

If you've made any promises, fulfill them.

Now let's try this with the other tool that will get the most work out of this expedition: your pen.

Go to your altar and take your comfortable position there. Take your pen in hand and notice the length and shape of it, the color. Feel the smoothness or the roughness of it. Click it if it is a ballpoint. If it is a fountain pen, admire the luster of the metal tip. Dip it, if you choose, and see the ink drip from it. Make some scratches on paper and see how smoothly it flows. Let yourself fall into the beauty of this simple tool that preserves words and experiences for the future.

Deep breaths. Close eyes. See the pen. Try to get a sense of the personality of this very important tool. Dashing romantic? Court reporter? Something else? Take your time to discover the spirit that inhabits this tool.

When you have that established, introduce yourself. Explain what you desire from your journey together. Listen for an answer. If you hear nothing, that's fine. Sometimes it takes time to make that connection. As above, if you hear a strong NO, choose another pen.

Take some time to chat a bit.

Then it will be time to return to the shared reality. Say goodbye to the spirit of the pen.

Open your eyes and use the pen to write down your experience. And, of course, if you've made any commitments, keep them.

———————

You can use this same technique for any of your secret country tools or, indeed, any tools at all. Try it with your hammer, your paintbrush, or your cookpot. It is truly an enriching experience to recognize those many levels of consciousness with whom we share this life.

———————

Take a few moments now to just relax and breathe in your experiences so far. The preparations have been lengthy, and the practices will be ongoing. You have been getting ready for the adventure of a lifetime that will last a lifetime. In fact, it has already begun. Do you feel eager for what is next? Are you nervous or excited to see what awaits you in your inner world? I hope there is a thrum of enthusiasm in you for this work. I hope that you have already felt the effects of your study and that your life has been enriched.

Part Two

THE
EXPEDITION

THE SANCTUARY

The Sanctuary is the first stop on this journey, and it is the most important. It is the beginning and the end of all that comes after.

Your Sacred Home

The Sanctuary is your personal sacred space, your perfect home on the astral plane (or in your imagination). It is the home of you as your own god, the personal deity that is your own highest self. Here you become more deeply aware of and connected to your Godself.

This is that part of you that remembers all it has been and done and seen before, the part that has the initial creation of your reality as its purpose in a spirit of joy and adventure. It is difficult to define in conventional terms. This is good! It keeps you from falling into preconceived notions and missing out on the beauty and truth of your singular self.

Godself holds the key to your destiny and answers the question: What are you here for? Your true will is living in your Godself throughout your life. There is no one else in all of time and space that can achieve your destiny for you. The way you find it is through your dedication to un-tangling complexes, cleansing wounds, re-breaking wrongly healed places and setting them properly this time. This might entail freeing yourself from what Starhawk has called "the wicked vow," that self-limiting prom-ise made in anger or frustration; e.g., "I will never speak to her again!" or "They won't have me to kick around anymore!" It might require sit-ting down with difficult people to resolve long-standing resentments. You might even need to release yourself from obligations that are draining you instead of feeding you.

What's the purpose of discovering your true will? Finding your true will brings the greatest joy and creative potential that you can have in this mortal life. There is a rightness to it that can inspire you through your darkest times and help you trust that your pain has some purpose. When I was in labor, giving birth to my daughter, the most helpful thing someone said to me was, "You're making progress." When your souls are in align-ment, you are always making progress, even when you feel completely stalled out. In alignment, you can trust that your impulses are healthy and will lead you where you need to go to continue moving forward. Your true will draws you to the people, the work, and the practices you need in your life.

Your Godself has the ability to change physical reality. This is already happening, according to your desires, fears, and expectations, as well as your Godself's higher wisdom. The beliefs you hold deep within are sent up to Godself, and if there's enough juice behind it, Godself will "make it so." You can see the manifestation of this principle most clearly when you have the same problems happening in your life over and over: no matter what car you drive, it breaks down; in every job, you have a coworker who lies about you; in every love relationship, you are betrayed. Clearly there's something deeper at work here; are you giving yourself this hard time?

Alternatively, you may experience great success in your endeavors: you have work you enjoy and you do it well; your love relationships are strong and solid; your transportation is infallible. Sometimes you can take credit for this awesomeness!

However, it's important to remember that no one lives in a vacuum (that would be too dusty!). We are all constantly cocreating this world with other beings and consciousnesses. The events of our lives reflect this inter-being. This means that even though your life might be hard right now, that doesn't necessarily indicate that you are out of alignment. Being fully yourself doesn't always equal ease. However, when you've been connecting to Godself regularly, you can be sure that whatever obstacles you are facing, you will be able to bring forth the gift from the exchange and move on from this challenge stronger. That doesn't always make it more fun, but hopefully it gives you hope that your struggles aren't in vain.

Also, you need to take into consideration that you are not always privy to what the gods, including your own Godself, have in store for you. At times, you must walk down a dark section of the path so you can get to the super cool clearing with astounding views. Other times you must lie in the shade and rest for a while, because you are soon going to meet a bear in the woods!

Godself operates with a greatly expanded view of time and a greater perspective on what is good for us. They are therefore much more willing than your other parts to put up with adversity. You can draw strength from this. When you are struggling, you can consider that part of your problem might be coming from what you expect, fear, and desire. But another part of it is that Godself looks at what is right for you in the long term. And they are willing to accept everything as an opportunity for growth and greater experience of life. As a wise friend says: aren't we lucky to be sensitive enough to feel pain and cold?

Sometimes folks say, "When you finally learn the lesson, the problem goes away on its own," which I think is only partly true. The spiral nature of our path often leads us into a new level of the same issue, so that we can continue to heal in deeper ways. In this way of thinking, there is no "final" to the "learning." What does it mean to "learn the lesson" of relationship? How do you know when you're done? Managing life is more like taking care of an orchard; you learn all you can and then each tree teaches you what it needs: protection from deer, more water, thinning of the fruit. It might be better to just take joy in the creativity of the lessons!

Godself operates on the same frequency as all other Godselves in the great family of Godselves. They are in constant communication with each other. You might think of it as a different dimension where all are connected, free of the bounds of time and space. When you send energy to another for healing or any other purpose, it's good to send through this channel; their Godself will decide what to do with your offering. There will be opportunities to practice this later on.

Generally, all forms of spirit communication are facilitated by a strong and open channel with Godself. When you are in alignment, you are ready to receive information and learn what to do with it. You are more capable, efficient, and powerful. You are less susceptible to being pulled off balance by messages you receive or the spirits you work with.

Godself is a source and a receiver of higher wisdom. You can tap into knowledge from arcane sources through a strong connection with Godself. Godself is timeless, like Fetch, but on a different level. Fetch is in the now because that's the limit of their understanding. Godself understands that all times are now, and the now is infinite. The feeling of oneness, grace, and enlightenment pour into you from Godself.

To support your relationship with Godself, *listen*. Use the tools most suited to this part of you. Sit in meditation; just take ten quiet minutes to breathe and let Godself speak to you. Practice divination: automatic writing, tarot, or bibliomancy. One school of thought says that divination works because of Godself's ability to manipulate reality, moving the card you need to see up to the top of the deck or moving your finger to the line of text you need to read. Whatever the mechanism, Godself will help you interpret what you receive in ways that are suited to your situation.

Another way to support your connection with Godself is to become willing to do the work you are led to do. This could be totally sweet and deeply enlightened work, or not. Many years ago, I was doing massage for a living, teaching Witchcraft, and participating in three or four major rituals a month. Most of the people I knew were on a strong spiritual path. I didn't understand why they got so upset in traffic or worried so much about mundane matters. Then I got a clear message that said, "Of course you don't have these issues; you are insulated. You need to learn to be in and of the world. Now's the time. See if your practices hold up out there." So I took a break from teaching and leading so many rituals. Then I seriously scaled back my massage practice and took a job installing security cameras. Talk about a change! And really not very fun at all. It wasn't what I imagined (or wanted) my spiritual practice to look like, but without it, I would have been only half-formed in my practices and teaching. So don't get stuck in what you think your path should look like. Be willing to have it be what it must be.

Ha Prayer for Integration

I invite you now to take a moment to do a short Ha Prayer with the purpose of settling in to what you're learning.

First, state your intention: May my understanding be of service to myself and the worlds.

Breathe: in-out-1, in-out-2, in-out-3, in-out-4, empowering your intention.

On 4, send the energy with a HAAAAAA or a hiss, a kiss, or a sigh up to your Godself.

Say: Let the rain of blessings fall.

In the Sanctuary, everything is oriented toward your comfort and ease. You may find yourself greeted by silence or wind chimes or Beethoven's

Ninth. You might see a well-lit room with a fireplace and full altar setup with stones and statues, or a simple space, dim and cool, with a single candle and a glass of water. Perhaps it looks like the backyard of your childhood home, or the grounds of your favorite retreat center.

It is rare for us to have the opportunity to make a place exactly how we want it, with no thought for anyone else. So enjoy this freedom. There is no need to stick to convention here, no need to wonder what the neighbors will think (they won't know anything!), or whether your partner will enjoy the overstuffed couch (it doesn't matter!). You are all that matters here.

And this is an important point: the Sanctuary is not the place to *become* anything. Too often, we are striving, trying to improve; we want to be thinner, smarter, more disciplined, and more successful. Leave that business at the door. The Sanctuary is the place to simply be what and how you already are. Don't come here to get better, faster, stronger. Come here to feel the embrace of all that you find comforting, to be held in the knowing of your own value. Come here to remember that, though you might seek change, you are already perfect. In this place, let there be no guilt! Don't bring in any "I should really sit up straighter" chairs or "I should really be doing daily meditation" charts. Bring only those things that help you remember that you are nothing less than an amazing, miraculous gift to the universe.

Of course, the point of a Sanctuary is that you can come to it when you feel pursued, trapped, or abused by outside or inside influences. You can come to it when you are overwhelmed and sad. You can come here, trusting that this place will never harm you. You will not be compared with others; you will not be judged. This place can handle your wild emotions, your anger, your breakdowns. You needn't fear destroying it accidentally because it is your Godself (who is always strong and whole and powerful) who maintains it.

Your visit to the Sanctuary comes first because you need to remember that you are a good being, flaws and all, and you must know that you have a place to go when you need healing and sustenance. You are worthy of these things, wherever you've come from, whatever you've endured on your way here. You deserve kindness and nurturing, especially from yourself.

You will notice that all of your journeys begin and end in the Sanctuary. This helps you to integrate what you've learned and to check in with yourself to see if you're ready for the next outing. Enjoy the changes that occur here, as you are yourself changed by your travels.

This is your private, secret, sacred home. Let it become second nature to come here and connect to your Godself, at peace and full of joy.

Visiting the Sanctuary

For this first journey, I am giving you a very long induction. In your future journeys, it will be much shorter. Use whichever feels necessary to you in the moment. Sometimes you will need a little extra time, especially if you've had a difficult day or something is weighing on your mind.

Listen to your breath. Let the rhythm of your breath be what it is. Quick and nervous, slow and languid, or in between. It might change because of your attention. Whatever it is is fine for now.

Feel the attention of you, the part that says, "What's that? What's this?" Let this noticing part become stronger. If these words mean nothing to you, or you're not sure what they mean, try this: say out loud, "What's that?" and see which part of your mind pops awake. If you're still not sure, that's fine; just let the ideas flow over you.

Direct your awareness to the top of your head. How's it feeling? Maybe you can't feel it at all. Touch it with your hands to guide your attention. Feel how your skin holds the echo of your fingers when you move your hand away. That's the top of your head. Let your mind's eye draw its shape. Visualize the hair follicles. If this is difficult, simply take a breath and say, "top of my head," take another breath and say, "top of my head," and then again. You can do this any time for any of these sections. If you are a word person, use words. If you are a kinetic person, touch the body part you are discussing. If you are visual person, visualize it. I do discourage you from using a mirror to literally see yourself; it's too easy to get stuck in judgments about appearance.

Okay, awareness at the top of the head. Breathe into that place. Just visualize the breath you take in going up there, filling your skull. You might see a glow beginning to appear where your breath is going. If you do, that's great; if not, that's fine too.

Take another breath and let your attention move down your skull. Breathe into your eyes and your eyebrows. Breathe into your ears. Breathe into your nose and mouth, your jaw. Let the glow increase.

Don't try to relax. Don't try to do anything. Just let breathing be what it is and direct it gently to these places in the body.

One big breath for the whole head.

Breathe into your neck. Feel the breath touching each vertebra. Observe any tightness and let it be. If you have pain, send a breath of acknowledgment there, then move on. Don't let yourself get stuck in it.

Breathe into your shoulders. If they are up around your ears, let them drop. Breathe into the space where shoulder and neck meet. Watch what the breath does here, what it wants to do.

Breathe into your upper arms, biceps, triceps. Attend to your elbows and let them fill with breath. Let another breath come into you and down your arms to your wrists, your hands. Shake them out if you are drawn to do that.

One big breath for your arms.

Another breath for the upper chest, front and back. Shoulder blades, pectorals. Be aware of your torso from all sides.

Breathe into your belly. You might feel tension here and desire to release it. Go ahead, if you want, but don't feel you must. Breathe your belly full of air and glow.

Breathe into your sex, your physical, subtle, or energetic genitals. Stay here for a while if you'd like, breathing, observing.

Big breath for your entire torso.

Breathe into your hips, those magical joints that allow you to walk and dance. Breathe into your butt on the chair, floor, or earth.

Breathe into your thighs, inner and outer, and breathe into strong muscles, weak, sore, whatever. It is what it is, for now. Start where you are.

Let a breath find its way to your knees. If you can't feel it, see it in your mind's eye, light and air flowing around and through the cartilage.

Let a breath find its way to your ankles and your feet. Witness the miracle of your bones in such intricate combination.

Big breath for your legs.

And let your attention move past your physical form and just a tiny bit into the earth. Feel the coolness there, the billions of microbes moving around your awareness.

Take just a breath or two feeling how your energy can expand beyond your physical form.

Then come back up from the earth and back into your own earthly body.

Back up through those clever joints and those meaty muscles. Up through all your darkness and richness.

Take a big, deep breath. Become aware of how this miracle of flesh moves on its own to take in the living air that enlivens you. Feel the air moving into you and out of you. Feel your body relax and soften as the rhythm of your breathing fills your awareness. Listen for your heartbeat, the blessed beating that has sustained you since your birth. Faithful heart, pushing the blood through your veins. Flow in the darkness of your body. Feel the blood of you feeding the bones of you, the frame on which your flesh hangs. A miracle of engineering, your magnificent body.

Your manifest self is your first temple, your first place of worship.

Now allow your awareness to come to stillness; feel it settle like water as the ripples of attention fade. And in that place of calm, let an image begin to form around you of the Sanctuary of your spirit. There is no need to rush to bring a vision forth. Simply let it come. If you are having trouble seeing anything, give yourself a head start by envisioning the safest, most beautiful place you've ever been. Personalize from that.

Know that this place is completely and entirely yours. No one is allowed to come here without your express permission. No one may disturb the harmony of this place.

Feel the position of your spirit body. Are you seated on the ground, on the floor, on the couch? Feel the dirt or the carpet or the leather beneath you.

Feel the air of this place touching your subtle skin. Is it warm or cool? Quick or still?

And notice, as you breathe in, whether there is any scent. Patchouli incense? Jasmine flowers? Spring rain?

Now let your sense of hearing come to the forefront. What sounds are here? Soft breeze rustling the trees? The songs of canary or nightingale? The rush of water? Music perhaps?

Take a breath and feel your body centered in your Sanctuary.

And finally, open your mind's eye and let your sense of sight come into play. What do you see? Shiny oak floors, Spanish tile, or Egyptian carpet? Painted murals on the walls, or Victorian wallpaper, or knotty pine paneling? Are there bookshelves? What titles are there? If your Sanctuary appears without doors and walls, what trees do you see here? Oak, redwood, sycamore? Are there flowers? Daisies, poppies, wild roses?

Now in your mind's eye, stand up and wander around. Look closer at any pictures or keepsakes you find. Locate the source of the music, if you can, and turn it up and down again. Is the lighting from electric lamps or candles? Blow the candles out and light them again. Dim the lights and turn them up. Touch things. Pick them up and look at them from all sides. If there are flowers, smell them.

Find your altar. If you don't yet have an altar in this place, begin to build one. Remember, this altar is a counterpart to your altar in the shared reality and becomes a bridge of sorts. See your cup here. Greet that spirit. See anything else you keep on your altar at home.

This whole space will become reflective of you and your journey as time goes on. This is where you will keep books you find at the Library, gifts you receive in the Shadow House, holy water you collect at the Temple. The Sanctuary will learn and grow with you.

Take ten minutes to wander about and see what there is to see. When it is time to return, call yourself back with a tone.

And come back to the cushion, chair, patch of grass where you began this exploration and sit. Close eyes. Come back to the breath. Let the breath you take in fill you and feed you. Let the breath you take in invigorate the cells of you and between the cells of you. And follow your breath into your body ... and out. And in ... and out. And once more, follow your breath into your body and back out into the space of light and noise, the shared reality. And when you are ready, open your eyes and be here now.

Sanctuary—Head, Heart, Hands

Remember in chapter 3 we talked about Head, Heart, and Hands activities? Here's your first chance!

Head: What Makes You Feel Safe?

- Work on the questions from your Travelogue pages (page 50), adding in these specifics to the Sanctuary:

  Is there any color dominant in the decor?

  Did you notice anything that made you smile immediately?

  Were you surprised by any objects you found there?

  Was there anything missing?

- Write for at least fifteen minutes, but more is better!

Heart: Songs of Fulfillment and Joy

- Find an hour's worth of music suited to playing in the Sanctuary. These should be songs that make you feel free, safe, and at ease. Make a playlist on your device, or a CD, and have that handy at your altar when you are doing your secret country work/play. Possibilities: Peter Gabriel's "Solsbury Hill," Kid Beyond's "I Shall Be Free," Genesis's "Keep it Dark," Great Big Sea's "Ordinary Day" …

Hands: Sanctuary Model/Collage

- Create an image of your Sanctuary using a collage, a painting, modeling clay, photos, or whatever you like.

- Using a sticky note, a pencil drawing, a photo, or other image, locate the Sanctuary on the map, as the very first place! Everything begins here and moves outward. Remember that the map is a rough draft and that you can revise it later if you change your mind about where things go (or change where things go in your mind).

The Gifts of Joy and Fulfillment

Each place that you go in the secret country has something to teach you. You learn not only from what you see and who you meet, but also from your own actions and reactions.

Here in the Sanctuary you are reminded that your fulfillment is important to the world. When you are in this state of grace, you are more focused. You have greater capacity to play and work and respond to whatever challenges arise. You spend less time opening the refrigerator door to see if anything new has appeared and more time in serene prayer or wild dancing or fierce activism—in other words, making the world a better place.

But what is fulfillment? It is an expression of your true self into the world, a satisfaction that goes both ways. Internal fulfillment means you know that you may not be perfect, but you are still good. External fulfillment means you know that the world is not perfect, but it is still good. You (and the world) are doing what you are here to do and being what you are here to be. This spurs a trust in your own worth. Fulfillment is self-respect, the desire to care for yourself as well as others. It shows up as equanimity, a sense of composure and ease. It gives you the ability to stay strong in the face of difficulty because no matter what is going on around you, you know that you are beautiful and strong. You can learn to remain centered in that truth.

Of course, this is not an easy task! There are all sorts of ways you might be sabotaged. You might judge yourself harshly for imagined failings and allow others' opinions to drive you to distraction. Self-love is what you're aiming for, but often you might struggle with mere self-acceptance.

We worked with some of this in the section on Values and Virtues. Remember thinking about what is truly important? Sorting out your priorities and bringing your integrity to the forefront of your life? This is a strong road to joy and fulfillment. Trusting yourself to make choices in alignment with the kind of world you want to live in gives you a good foundation. You can see objectively how your presence makes the world a better place.

Truly valuing yourself and your pleasures is not the same as narcissism. In fact, it's quite the opposite. Where the self-obsessed person wants all the attention for themselves, the one who understands their true merit has no need for that outside validation. An understanding of your inherent worth is a good way to prevent overweening pride and arrogance.

To sum up, spending time in your Sanctuary surrounded by beauty and comfort is a good way to remember your right place in the world.

Roadblocks to Joy and Fulfillment

Take a minute right now to stop reading and think about joy and fulfillment. What does it mean to you? If you have big challenges coming up in you, "Put them in the cup!"

Now let's talk a bit more about joy and what that means.

It's not always what you would think of as "happiness." Sometimes it's simply a sense of rightness, the sense that everything is as it should be, imperfect and broken as the world is and you are. In its highest expression, it feels like grace, a feeling of oneness, a gift from god, the universe, the cosmic I AM.

Joy can be activated by physical sensation: opening to the warmth of the sun on your face, hearing the voice you've been longing to hear. You might feel a deep sense of joy when you return from your secret country wanderings and feel again the delicious heaviness of your flesh.

Joy can also come from your emotional state: feeling the deepening of a friendship as you share stories of happiness and sorrow, the spreading of goodwill as you do meditation practice, the hopefulness that you feel as you watch brave souls confronting injustices. These happen in the shared reality, as well as in the inner worlds. Your connection with your allies, your shadows, and your ancestors can give you this sense of rightness.

Your joy and fulfillment are your birthrights. Not all-the-time happiness or I'm-so-perfect-ness, but contentment with your life and yourself. I believe this. As cells in the body of God (or organisms in the ecosystem of Gaia), we all get to be healthy and whole. We are each precious; we each have a part to play.

This is why you have this capacity for full-throated laughter, and orgasm, and mad dancing! This is why you can feel the simple appreciation of a kind word or warm welcome. You have the power to embrace your own fulfillment and to help provide those experiences for others.

Back at the beginning I said I wasn't going to ask you to "believe" anything in this book, but I changed my mind. Please believe me when I say that *you are worth more to the world when you are loving yourself and taking care of your own joy*. Again, not the pretend kind of joy that's really a result of addiction or other short-term satisfactions, but true-heart joy, the kind that sends your heart spinning in love or opens a fit of laughter in you or inspires a song of delight.

I implore you: seek opportunities to do what makes you happy. If you love to dance, please do dance, here and there and everywhere! If you love to lay in a hammock and read, do that. If something that other people might call drudgery makes you feel good, do it and whistle while you work.

Two of my favorite practices for feeling valuable and joyous are blessing and gratitude.

BLESSING

Blessing is a generous contribution to the well-being of ourselves and others. There is something in us that desires this. Humans, and many other creatures, are built for building each other up. First, babies are selfish, then they learn to share, then they want to share! I encourage you to set free your own desire to share.

Learn to recognize a blessing, to offer a blessing, to internalize the concept of blessing so deeply that it becomes second nature. Choose a blessing mindset.

Things and experiences are attracted to you because of the energy you surround yourself with and what you focus on. It's not as simple as "The Law of Attraction" would have you believe, by any means, but your attitudes do affect those around you and how they feel about you and how you feel about yourself. When you choose to offer goodwill into the world, you make yourself open to receive the same in return. You become inclined to allow more positive interactions.

Now, to be clear, sometimes it is obvious that the cards are stacked against you, especially if you are part of a disenfranchised population. When you are called to fight injustice, you must fight. This doesn't mean you should abandon your principles. Martin Luther King, Jr. was a very effective leader without becoming hateful and intolerant like those he opposed.

Interestingly, blessings can include those things that feel difficult at first but hold some sort of secret benediction: a "blessing in disguise." These are harder to recognize until you get a little distance, but many things that were troubling at the time gave you tools and gifts that you needed later.

So how to practice blessing?

Bless the one who has a thing you want. Offer a little prayer of "Good job! You got the thing!" If you can't do that, bless the thing itself first. If you can't do that, maybe there's an issue with the thing or with your wanting. Listen to your words as you talk about the situation. Check in with that. Are you envious? Do you want to make less of it, sour-grapes style? Are you angry? Disdainful? Resistant?

Those feelings are understandable. When fortune strikes and allows someone else to have something you always wanted, it's hard to stay out of negativity. That's why blessing is a practice, because sometimes it's really hard! Putting those feelings in the cup is a good way to deal with resentments. Having a conversation with the object of your difficulty can also be helpful.

Bless those who are having a harder time than you. Offer condolences, a shoulder to cry on, or a casserole. Spend time listening. Offer a ride to the store or the doctor. If you are lucky enough to have a place of relative peace, give safe haven to those who need it.

Guilt can be a good helper in this process, but only as a pointer to what you think or feel. Use your guilt as a guide, then dispense with it.

It's like pain: when it has given its message, its job is done. Put your guilt in the cup.

Bless those who make you mad. Do that with a "May you be blessed with awareness of your own highest good" prayer (not a "F**k you" prayer, which, yes, is also a prayer, only the unhelpful kind).

There is a Buddhist practice in which you first allow your heart and mind to fill with love and compassion for a loved one, then a respected teacher or mentor, then a neutral person, then a person you really don't like. This powerful practice helps free you from resentment. This quote from Anne Lamott describes the danger of hanging on to a grudge: "Not forgiving is like drinking rat poison and then waiting around for the rat to die." Don't poison yourself. Find your inner calm, then make your action direct and sure, as necessary.

Loving-Kindness Blessing Practice

Take a deep breath and allow the breath you take in to fill you and feed you. Allow your physical form to soften, your muscles to relax. Drop your shoulders. Let an image come into your mind of a moment of great happiness, centered on someone you love very much. See their smile, hear their voice. Become deeply aware of how your heart feels, open and connected. Let that feeling encircle you so you are surrounded by a sphere of gently glowing light. Remember that this is a very specific kind of energy, one that elevates and empowers a person's highest being, through the grace of your Godself and theirs. You are not just offering your power to them to do with as they please.

Take several breaths with this vision. Then allow an image to arise of a mentor or teacher, someone who has helped you become a better person, whatever that means to you. Remember the times you succeeded because of this person's help, and choose the one that makes you proudest. Let your heart expand with goodwill. Again, take several breaths with this vision.

Then allow an image to come forth of an acquaintance, someone you have neutral feelings about. This might be a person who rides the bus with you each day or the barista who serves your coffee. Take them into the circle of your loving-kindness. See them smiling with the good feeling of your blessing. Again, take several breaths with this vision.

Finally, bring into your mind a person who you really have trouble with. This might be a politician or a former boss or partner. Note: this is really hard to do! Remember to relax your body. Let tensions go. See if you can hold the circle of goodwill and allow this person to enter in. Maybe for now, you just let them stand at the edge of the circle and feel a tiny bit of the glow. Maybe next time you will let them closer, if you choose. When you are ready to stop this exercise, allow your loving-kindness to be drawn back into your center, so that you are also blessed.

Do this practice daily for maximum benefit.

GRATITUDE

In blessing, you experience give and take, and for this, you can have gratitude. Take a moment right now to consider what you are grateful for. Are you safe in your home? Are you well fed? Healthy? Maybe your answer to these questions is no. Then go deeper. Are you breathing well? Do you have all your fingers and toes? Can you read? (I bet you can!)

Gratitude is energy. It fuels change and growth. It connects you with the giver (who- or what-ever that might be) and helps you hold your place as a cell in the body of God. For everything that is given to you, you can give, at least, your gratitude and thus allow the energy to continue to flow. It is not easy, especially as a new mission. But if you practice, change will happen. You will get better at seeing not only the things that are wrong in the world, but also the things that are right.

A strong gratitude practice can include:

- Saying grace before a meal. Many religious (and nonreligious) traditions have a form of expressing appreciation for your food and the hands that picked it, prepared it, cooked it. If you are a meat eater, say thank you to the chicken or the cow that gave its life to sustain yours.

- Saying prayers of thanksgiving each morning and evening. In the morning, you might be grateful for a good night's sleep or a safe bed. If you don't have those things, what is there in your life that you can speak morning prayers about? In the evening, give thanks for your day, the people who graced it, the small moments of warmth or kindness.

- Showing appreciation to those around you. When someone helps you, say thank you. If you have a good experience with customer service, tell them all the ways that they made your life easier and how glad you are. When you get off the bus, say thank you to the driver.

- Again, just like in your blessing practice, there are times that you will be in great hardship. Things are just crappy. People are sick and tired and broken. Floods, fires, and other catastrophes occur. Sometimes you lose everything except your own breath and heartbeat. For all its beauty, life can be cruel. And still, here you are, with a choice of how to act. When you're done screaming and crying (and there is definitely a time and place for that), you can go outside and be grateful that the sun still rises and sets each day.

- Taking the long view is one way to appreciate the circumstances that feel hard right now. You can see how your struggles and your pains fit into the overall picture of your life, by looking backward at those situations that have shaped you, without which you would not be. You can also look at what you can see coming and consider how these things might serve you in the long term.

Here's a variation on the loving-kindness meditation that will help you get used to expressing gratitude:

Loving-Kindness Gratitude Practice

Take a deep breath and allow the breath you take in to fill you and feed you. Allow your physical form to soften, your muscles to relax. Drop your shoulders.

Let an image come into your mind of a moment of great happiness centered on someone you love very much. See their smile, hear their voice. Say "thank you" to them. Name the reasons why you are thankful for their presence in your life.

Next, allow an image to arise of a mentor or teacher, someone who has helped you become a better person, whatever that means to you. Express your gratitude to this person in detail.

Then allow an image to come forth of an acquaintance, someone you have neutral feelings about. This might be your postal carrier or someone in your English class. Thank them for the smile or the kind word.

Let's not invite the person you have serious trouble with yet. First you must figure out what is the gift in that situation (there often is one, probably well hidden). Maybe the gift is simply increased fortitude. Once you've got that sorted, saying "thank you" to them will free up all sorts of energy for you.

When you are ready to stop this exercise, say "thank you" to yourself for taking the time to make the world a more grateful place!

Again, do this practice daily for maximum benefit.

Dreams and Visions—The Unbidden Contact

The Sanctuary is a specific place in the secret country of yourself, which you purposefully visit to be reminded of your true worth. But the secret country can also reach out and tap you on the shoulder for attention. This can happen through your night dreams, daydreams, bursts of creative inspiration, or psychic hits. The primary thing these all have in common is that you don't necessarily go looking for them. And occasionally they are pretty scary! They appear on their own and then what do you do?

First, remember what you learned in the Sanctuary: your joy and ful-fillment are required for your health and ability to affect positive change in the shared reality. Do an Untangling Rite to clear your mind. Do a Ha Prayer to align your souls. Remember that even if these shoulder taps point you toward tasks you know will be difficult, they still could be an-gels pointing you toward god.

There is a lot of overlap between dreams and visions, and to be clear, they aren't always something you see. A vision might involve hearing music that wants to be written or smelling a scent that is asking to be made a perfume. If you are synesthetic, it can get quite complicated!

We tend to call something a dream when we believe it isn't real and a vision when we suspect that it is. We only rarely get to know for sure which of these is true. And in the secret country, it really doesn't matter.

So let's talk first about dreams. There are many different ideas about what a dream actually is. Is it a way for your mind to process all the infor-mation that it has ignored during the day? A playground for possibility? A window into another reality? Any or all of these might be true.

In a way, the secret country work is like lucid dreaming, the prac-tice of staying conscious of oneself during REM sleep. They both have to do with managing situations in a realm that is outside the shared reality. Knowing that you're dreaming can help you manipulate outcomes in the dream state.

Lucid dreaming is a skill that takes a lot of practice, and even then some of us just aren't good at it. Like me, for instance. I have a vibrant dream life but have yet to master being in control in that realm. I can, however, pick up a dream circumstance and go work it out in the secret country.

The biggest problem when working with dreams is that they tend to get lost quickly when you wake up. To help with this issue, keep a dream journal next to your bed and write down your dreams immediately upon waking, or as much as you can remember. If you can get down the most important images or feelings from the dream, you might be able to pull it all back in when the time comes.

Daydreams are similar to night dreams but are usually more coherent, less apparently random. They're those free-form mental meanderings that happen when you're bored in class or a meeting goes on and on. Part of your mind checks out of the shared reality and begins to open to other possibilities. It might start with remembering the concert you went to last night, the people you were with, how you were dancing. This memory turns into something else when you begin to see events that didn't actually happen in the shared reality but you wish they did. Or you see things you feared would happen, or some combination of the two.

These reveries can be visions of delight or discomfort, depending on how your mind is drawn. Some folks are plagued with persistent thoughts; if that's you, I invite you to supplement your secret country work with some good ol' fashioned therapy, preferable with someone who will credit your spiritual inclinations. Some folks have a hard time keeping their mind on what's happening in front of them, and they're always in trouble for being too dreamy. If you have this issue, consider why. Perhaps what's happening in front of you is not in line with your service to yourself or the world. If that's the case, your dreaminess might be leading you to a change of occupation or scenery. Of course, it's not always easy to just pick up and go; maybe what you're daydreaming about is how to make it possible for yourself to change jobs or living situations!

Memory Play

Think back to a time when you felt safe, warm, content. Find a dream or a memory that brings a smile to your face. Allow yourself to really inhabit this vision, feeling the sunlight or hearing the rain. Now let your mind wander to what else might have been happening around you, things you couldn't know. What show was on the TV in the other room? Who was washing dishes? What creatures were roaming around outside? Let your mind play with this for a while. No expectation of rightness is needed. Here you are just exploring the edge between dream and vision.

Visions don't only come to those with strong psychic gifts. You might find yourself suddenly seeing your grandma pick up a phone and wonder what it means. I'd interpret that as her trying to get in touch with you. If she is still living, give her a ring. If she's passed beyond the veil, do some divination and pay her a visit in the secret country.

When you've had a dream or vision that you're interested in further pursuing, try the following exercise.

Dreams and Visions Exercise

Go to your altar. Close your eyes. Breathe. Let the breath you take in fill you and feed you. Let the breath you take in vitalize your elegant mind, your animal body, the starry crown of your divinity. Relax and come into your trance state. Find yourself in your Sanctuary. Take a few breaths to get centered in your souls' sacred, private home.

Open your physical eyes. If this pertains to a night dream, read over your dream journal. If it's a psychic hit you are trying to suss out, look at your notes. Close your eyes to see your Sanctuary, and open them as needed to look at your words. Think about your situation. What is your purpose? Is it just to find out what happens? Or is it to guide the incident to a better resolution than what you experienced? Is this a place you want to keep in your secret country? Or are you happy to have it disappear as soon as you've completed your tasks here? Either way is fine, and, as always, it's your choice. Call for your guardian to join you, if you want.

There may be items that you need to take with you to face whatever awaits; gather them here from your stash. Holy water, trade goods, a magick flower, or a bottle of wine might help you resolve your difficulties. I do strongly caution you to not bring violence into the secret country. Your best course of action in dealing with a nightmare is a binding against further harm. Envision the interloper in a room with strong locks, or chained up, or otherwise kept from further violence. You might envision them shrinking down until they are as tiny as a mouse, or growing younger and younger until they are a baby. Then they have a second chance to do a better job of growing up!

Now let your spirit body rise from its comfortable place in the Sanctuary and go to the door. In a moment you will find yourself in the dream or vision, ready to take whatever action is required. Open the door and step through.

Take stock of your surroundings. If you do not recognize the surroundings, open your physical eyes again and look at your writing. Get as strong a sense of it as you can, then close your eyes again. If you still don't find yourself where you expected to be, call for your guardian and wait right there until they appear. Do a Ha Prayer to align and ask Godself to guide you. Then, step forth with confidence.

When you are finished with your work or play, go back to your Sanctuary. Be at rest there. Let yourself be nurtured by your own beauty once more before you rejoin the shared reality.

More Magick at the Sanctuary

The Sanctuary is a great place to work personal magicks. Here are a few powerful ways to boost your meditations and spell work.

First, getting your Three Souls on board with the magickal plan means that there is no part of you that is hesitant or resisting your success. You tap the unique abilities of your mind, body, and spirit to make a plan and carry it out, with a big dose of divine blessing. Et voilà! It is done!

Second, make sure that you are not holding yourself back with your confusion or disquiet by doing a strong cleansing spell. The Untangling Rite is part of this, of course, but you can also do cleansing baths or even clean out your whole workspace if you find that something's not quite right with your juju.

Next, gather your spell components: herbs, oils, stones, charms, cloths, candles. Take a moment with all these things before you and do the "Talking to Your Tools" exercise from chapter 4. Call forth the unique spirits attached to the physical objects before you. Invite them to help you with your desired outcome.

Assuming everyone is on board (if they're not, find a substitution that's amenable!), it's time to work your spell. The instructions for these will vary, but the most important thing remains the same: working in partnership with the spirits of your components in a respectful way.

As an example, let's start with that cleansing spell.

When it comes to cleansing, water is your friend, though fire is also good for deep work. Important to note: when you do this kind of cleansing work, *it doesn't necessarily make things go away*. Sometimes it just takes the hooks out of you so that you can choose how you want to engage with things. You are no longer compelled.

Cleansing Bath
HERE'S WHAT YOU NEED:
Salt (about ¼ cup)

Lavender flowers (a handful)

2 tealights

A quart-sized jar (or similar) of water

A small basin (a baking pan will do)

HERE'S WHAT YOU DO:
Now, this spell takes place at sunrise (yes, that is very early!), so you'll want to start the evening before with your preparations.

First, perform the Ha Prayer for Triple-Soul Alignment on page 28.

Then, because this is a cleansing spell itself, the pre-cleansing step can be shortened to simply washing your hands and speaking words like, "I wash away what keeps me from being fully present in this moment."

Have before you the salt, flowers, candles, and jar of water. Take a pinch of salt and put it on your tongue. Invite the spirit of salt to be with you. Can you get an image of them? A sense of their personality? It's fine if you can't just yet. Salt is almost always amenable to cleansing work!

Pick up the lavender flowers and roll them in your hands just a bit to release their scent. What does it bring to mind? Do you have any memories associated with this smell? If those memories are pleasant, then lavender is a good choice for you. If not, you might use rosemary leaves instead. Ask the spirit of the plant to be with you in this working.

Light the tealights for just long enough that the flame begins to draw the wax up the wick, and then put them out. Pay attention to the moment that happens, as it indicates whether the candles are aligned with your purpose. If your candles won't stay lit long enough to do this, either use different ones or try to figure out why. Sometimes you can fix a recalcitrant candle by "splinting" the wick with a cut-off bit of another wick.

Finally, see how the clear water fills the jar. There is no place that water withdraws from; it resists nothing. Take a small sip and enjoy the refreshment. Invite the spirit of water to be with you.

Next, pour the salt into the water. Swirl it around and let it dissolve.

Roll the flowers in your hand again to help release their scent and drop them into the water.

Place the two unlit candles in front of the jar and leave it overnight.

In the morning, get up before sunrise.

Take your jar of water with the salt and flowers in it along with the tealights and the basin into the bathroom.

Set the tealights to the sides of the tub or shower so that you will step between them when you step out.

Light the candles.

Set the jar of salt water and the basin so that you can reach them.

Take a regular shower.

When you're all clean, turn off the water and place the basin between your feet, or stand in it.

Take the jar of water and, starting with the top of your head, pour it over you, brushing with your other hand, brushing off all those old stories.

You may choose to ask the gods for help, the saints, or whoever else you might pray to, including your own higher power or Godself.

After you've poured out all the water, step out of the tub/shower, between the candles, which have made a "gate" for you to step into your day, cleansed and cleared.

You may speak a prayer here, acknowledging that you step into a new day, fresh and clean. Perhaps something like, "I cast off the ills of the past and move into a bright future!"

Let yourself air-dry (you don't want to wipe off the protective power of your spell!).

Dress yourself and reach back into the tub/shower and bring out the basin of yucky water.

Take it off your property. It's traditional to leave it at a crossroads, but I generally prefer to work with a helpful tree. Too much salt can be a big problem for growing green things, but usually a little bit won't hurt them. Just be polite and make sure you ask first. Often a tree is your best ally for turning your old yuckiness into something useful.

(You can also make a connection with the tree itself, in the secret country, and talk to them about it.)

Then, get on with your awesome day!

Planting Intentions

This is a spell that introduces a slightly different take on the relationship between your secret country and the shared reality.

HERE'S WHAT YOU NEED:

3 fava beans (aka "mojo beans" or "wishing beans")

Potting soil

A small plant pot

Water

HERE'S WHAT YOU DO:

Have all your components before you.

Take your beans in hand. Recognize that these are living things in stasis. Let your vision soften, and see these seeds in all their potential and possibility. See if they have any sort of personality that you can connect to. Sometimes a seed will carry a sort of memory of their parent plant, or a nascent disposition that you can approach.

Breathe your way into your Sanctuary, still holding the beans. See a door there and step through. Find yourself in a lovely garden.

Tell the beans what you'd like to grow in your life: money or love or luck or business success. Tell all three the same thing. Ask for their assistance.

Plant them in the soil of your garden at the Sanctuary, and also in the physical dirt in the pot. Keep in mind the minute lifeforms that inhabit dirt and ask for their blessing on your spell. Alternatively, you can plant them outside, but then you're limited by season.

Gift the seeds with water, recognizing the power of this element to soften and awaken them. Each day, take a moment to visit your Sanctuary garden and see how they are growing. Also, watch them in the shared reality. If they are not doing well for whatever reason, see if you can connect with the spirit of the plant to understand what they need. If not, google it! Or ask a gardener. Consider that everything you do in the physical realm influences your working: less water, more sun, a bigger pot, more support for the growth of the plant. Think about how these are metaphors for how you work emotionally, intellectually, physically.

And know that a magickal working is only one aspect of growing what you want in your life. Don't forget to make the call, read the note, answer the message, or send the résumé. In other words, do the footwork!

Sending Energy from Godself to Godself

We talked back in chapter 2 about sending energy from your Godself to another's. Here's one way to do that.

Start at your altar, as usual. Breathe your way into your Sanctuary.

Now, envision what kind of energy you'd like to send to your intended target. Maybe a friend has asked for healing an illness, courage for a court case, or strength to resist an abuser. Whatever you want to send, see that energy filling your hands with light. Healing often appears as a blue glow, courage as orange, strength as red or brown. Think about your motivation for wanting to do this. If it's muddy, do the Untangling Rite until you can be clear in your sending. Let the energy become discrete, with clear edges, until it forms into two jewels you can hold in your hand.

Go to the door and step outside. Find yourself in the garden again, and call for a bird to come to you. Maybe you draw them with a handful of seeds or by whistling to them.

When the bird arrives, ask them if they are willing to carry something for you. If they agree, then first give them the "address" by envisioning the person you're sending it to. Once you're sure they have it, give them one of the jewels. Watch them fly away and trust that they will deliver your gift to where it belongs.

Keep the second jewel in a safe place in your Sanctuary. This is your own touchstone to keep tabs on the situation. With this item, you can continue to support your friend by filling it up with power that will also fill its twin. When the magick is done, the healing is complete, the case is decided, and the abuser is dealt with, bury the jewel in the garden to release the rest of its energy out into the world.

Again, you may also choose to create these jewels of power in the shared reality by starting with stones or crystals that are of the same material: two bits of fluorite for healing, citrine for courage, carnelian for strength. This works especially well if the two stones were once one. Charge them using the same visualization and send one of the stones to your friend in the shared reality.

— *Six* —
THE SHADOW HOUSE

*N*ow you've spent some time basking in your own beauty and tranquility. You have gotten oriented in the best parts of yourself. It's been lovely, but the Sanctuary is only the starting place. There is so much more to see and experience.

You move now into purposeful seeking of your deepest darkness. You move now toward your Shadow House.

———

Meeting the Darkness

The Shadow House is another aspect of the Sanctuary; between them they hold the innermost core of who you are, the best and the worst of you, your greatest hopes and deepest fears. In one you see your value and find fulfillment; you celebrate your accomplishments. In the other, you gird yourself to face hatred, misery, and pain in those parts of you that you have banished from your sight. In both places you learn to rely on your Godself. They are neither two ends of a spectrum nor two sides of a coin; they feed and complement each other in all ways.

The Shadow House can be frightening, of course. You may fear even getting close to it. That is excellent! That feeling of apprehension means that there is much to be reclaimed within those walls. There is plenty of work for you, and *you can do this*. By aligning your souls, putting your fears into the Untangling cup, and staying connected to your support networks, you can resolve the issues that have been draining your power.

Our shadows are entities for whom we are responsible. We made them, or they were made for us, through no fault of their own. Since then, they have been hidden away with the hope that they'd never be seen again. It is time to advance a rescue mission to bring them back into the fold!

Depending on your personal experience, in the House you may find the shadow of the five-year-old who was shamed for showing his penis to the girls in class, the ten-year-old that never told on the neighbor for lighting the fire that burned the house, the twenty-year-old who slept with all her friends' boyfriends as a twisted show of power. You may find the dreamer who was told his dreams were crazy, the artist who hasn't painted since her father told her that artists are bums, the passionate lover who is unwilling to admit to the kind of love he desires. Do you see the connection? It is shame and embarrassment, rage and distrust, sadness and vulnerability that generate shadows. The denizens of the Shadow House are as unique as you are, but you can believe that as human creatures living life on earth, we share many in common.

There are many kinds of shadows: thought patterns, behaviors, unwelcome feelings. Talker and Fetch generate their own sorts of shadows, and their misinterpretation of Godself is another source of trouble. Talker shadows are overly analytical, obsessively atheistic, stuck in old thought patterns, and unwilling to experience the metaphysical world. Fetch shadows show up as laziness, ignorance of social mores, being intensely reactionary, and acting out. You might interpret Godself's objectivity as a shadow. Because they experience life on such a grand scale, they might appear unsupportive of your daily concerns. That's probably a little bit true.

Godself has limited allegiance to the day-to-day. They mean to remind you to expand your vision.

There are shadows that come from your family or community of origin. These are often hard to uproot because they were planted by someone you were taught to trust. There are others that you pick up along the way through your own experiences; these may make sense in the moment but are often a result of complexes that offer a false sense of understanding. For instance, you may have had isolated contacts with problematic people and concluded that all bosses are manipulative or all doctors are cruel.

Then there are those shadows that are formed because someone at some point told you that it's not okay to love who you love, to express yourself dramatically, or to fight for your beliefs. Anytime you go against the values of the common culture, you risk generating shadows. This doesn't mean you shouldn't do it. It simply means that intentionality is important as a part of your evolution, as is being as honest and clear as possible.

There will be things you find in the darkness that aren't scary and mean. You are likely to find some lights under bushels in the House, shadows of power and beauty. Consider this: many women were told when they were young that they were too opinionated, too loud, too big for their britches. Many women have chosen to tuck away that confident and self-assured girl that they were in favor of complying with society's desires. That is power hidden away. Many men were told when they were young that it wasn't manly for them to play with dolls or style their hair. Many men have chosen to disappear that darling young man that they were. That is beauty disguised.

One of the best outcomes of shadow work is the reclaiming of those parts of yourself whose freedom will truly bring you joy!

Of course, not all shadows are positive and helpful. Some were generated by deeds that you are ashamed of, that you regret, that make you feel powerless and angry. They rise from your bad behaviors or others bad behaviors. They are beliefs that serve only to keep you paranoid and fearful.

Shadows have issues: fear of abandonment, distrust, rage. They are racist and homophobic and cruel. Scared and hurt and desperate. They mess up your magick, derail your plans, shunt your energy in the wrong direction. While you're up here doing love spells, they're back there doing no-love spells! The shadows shield you from your desires because of some misguided protective instinct. They tell you that you don't deserve good things in your life.

And you are not alone in this. All of us, for our own reasons, hide our mistakes, our fears, our dislikes and likes. Maybe we want the world to think we're always perfect, always smart, always brave, always making right choices. We might be fooling everyone, including ourselves. We might act like we don't see the truth or don't feel it. We might think we're working from a clear understanding, but we're not. We're acting out of a fear that our grandmother gave us, of those people. We're living out our uncle's model of using violence to solve problems. We're playing out a vision that not only has no real investment in for us, but is also a detriment to the world.

I encourage you to become aware of how your shadows are affecting your life. Notice when you have a repeating thought pattern that makes you uncomfortable, makes you lose your temper, or makes you avoid situations because of your fear. Go to the Shadow House with the intention of finding the stories that are generating those behaviors. Recognize, hear, and claim these stories. With practice, you might find yourself doing this reflexively, which is difficult in the moment, but it is much healthier in the long run!

One way to keep rooted in your commitment is to do the "Running Your Values Pentacle" exercise from back in chapter 2. If you do this as a daily practice, it will go a long way toward orienting you in the direction of your desires. Remember to follow through the whole practice of drawing the boundary between what is you and what is not you. Then use that shield of your values whenever you have need of protecting yourself.

The Demons: Problems with Personalities

Sometimes a little shadow work goes too long undone and solidifies. You've avoided something beyond the point where a simple visit to the Shadow House will suffice. Or, possibly you have experienced a severely traumatic event, or an ongoing series of smaller injuries. In any of these cases, your problem can grow a personality of sorts. It gives rise to what I would call a demon. Remember, the difference between angels and demons is only that one points toward god and the other points away. The demon would rather you continue to be unwell; they are opposed to your healing. They do not have your best interests at heart.

Here's how it usually works. Something bad happens. This could be something done to you or something you did. It's horrid. Nasty. Ugly. You dissociate from it. You create a special place for it, a locked room in your Shadow House. In that room, the story just replays and replays. The demon watches the door and keeps everyone away.

If you are not careful, you can easily fall in love with your demons. If they are strong, generated by a feeling of superiority, they are powerful and good-looking. If they are weak, a victim of someone else's bad behavior, they are precious and needing protection. Think about whether you are supporting these creatures in your life. Are you continuing to listen to them, seeking food for them that they will find nourishing, trying to avoid hurting their feelings? Are you inviting experiences into your life that sustain them? Your demons are part of you, but it takes a tremendous amount of energy to keep them alive, energy you could certainly put to a better use.

Whether dealing with a shadow or a demon, the healing begins in the same way: by seeking them out. Shadow work is easier than demon work because shadows are less substantial, although that can also make them harder to see. Use statements of intention, such as, "I go forth with courage and compassion to hear the stories I have lost. May I be blessed in this undertaking."

Craft a ritual, large or small, creating talismans as keys to remembering your intention. Divination is excellent for finding out where the shadows are hiding and how to deal with them. And, of course, psychological counseling is helpful.

Remember, the more you are "there" attending to old issues, the less you are "here" attending to your current situation. The goal of this purposeful search is to know yourself, to love yourself, to fully inhabit yourself and your life. This reclaiming of personal power is one of the greatest gifts you can give and receive.

DEMONS VS. SHADOWS

Take a moment to consider the difference between demons and shadows. Do you have any specific situations in your life that may have generated one of those fierce protectors? Do you feel safe to confront it? If you are struggling with severe trauma, it is best to get help from a doctor or therapist so you don't have to go it alone.

Visiting the Shadow House

Go to your altar and begin with the breath. Let the breath you take in fill you and feed you. Let the breath you take in invigorate the cells of you, and between the cells, the emptiness that is you. Breathe into your center, into that still point within you, that place of restful, peaceful calm. Breathe into that place and let it expand around your consciousness. As always, start in your Sanctuary.

Let an image begin to form around you of your most precious home in the secret country of yourself. Rest easy for several moments here.

Now, send out a call for your guide and guardian, your ally, the one you connected to back in chapter 4. This particular foray will take you to a more dangerous place, and it will be good to have someone with you. It is time to find what is hidden and interact with those parts of you that you thought you might never see again. They are part of you, and you can reclaim them, and in doing so, reclaim your life-force.

Begin by declaring your intention: I go forth with courage and compassion to hear the stories I have lost. May I be blessed in this undertaking. And again. And once more. The magick of repetition is helpful here, and three times is the charm.

Rise up now in your subtle body and go to the door. Open the door and find a pathway there, leading into a stretch of woods, very near.

(Maybe the last time you were here, this was a sweet meadow, but things change quickly in the secret country, and it is your desire and willingness that creates it. Today you do shadow work, so the land creates the appropriate setting.)

The forest is dark and forbidding, but you are strong, and your ally is with you, and together you move forward. You walk a while through the cool air and see how the sunlight drifts weakly through the trees, casting weird shadows on the ground. Strange noises surround you, chittering and raucous chirping.

Finally, you come to a clearing with a powerful sphere of protection around it. In the center of the clearing, you see your Shadow House.

What does it look like? A hovel? A mansion? A prison or a cave? This place is called the Shadow House because it is home to the shadows, but it may not look like a traditional house.

Feel in your body your fear or discomfort, your anticipation and determination.

Recognize that this is your place, all of it. You created the whole forest and this sphere of protection to keep everyone away, including yourself. Think of the strength it took to build this and the energy it takes to maintain it. Think what you could do if that energy was freed up for you to put toward your desires instead of your fears.

Now, step up to the barrier of energy, the force field that surrounds this place. It looks impenetrable, and it is to everyone but you. Using the same power with which you created it, make for yourself a door that only opens at your hand. Step forth into the clearing. Again, state your intention: I go forth with courage and compassion to hear the stories I have lost.

Take another deep breath and step to the door of the Shadow House.

Reach for the doorknob. Is it locked? Do you have a key? Or does your ally?

Maybe you don't have a key and right now you don't want to. Maybe this is too soon for you to face what might be awaiting you in the Shadow House. That's okay. Maybe for now you can just look at it from afar. Next time, you may open the door. The time after that, you may go inside. And so on. It's important to remember that it is always up to you how far you go.

In this case, I will assume that you do enter the darkened space. What do you see? If this is like a house, you might see the usual types of furniture, like bookcases or chairs. If it appears as a cave, you might see a fire pit surrounded by rocks. If a prison, you might see cells. Take a moment to look around.

Keep moving through this place until you come to a hall lined with many doors. Here, you see words or images describing who or what might be inside the rooms. You might find "elementary school" or "best friends" or "swim team" or something else that makes sense only to you. Go to any of these.

Take a breath. Restate your intention if you wish. If you are very afraid, run your Values Pentacle again and keep your shield with you.

Enter the room. As you step through the door, see a long, black slip of dark that extends from your foot to a figure standing within. It is an image of you, a shadow-form.

Remember that this is all you, in every part, and that you have the ultimate power over what happens here. Take a breath, find a place of comfort, and sit with your shadow. Invite them to tell you a story of something you'd forgotten or denied for too long, something that you've locked away.

Listen with compassion for yourself. Try your best to hold good thoughts for this shadow, bravely revealing themselves to you, being vulnerable. Forgive them, if it is in you to do so.

There is no need to resolve anything now, only to hear this part of you that has been kept silent. Allow the story to come into you and allow your shadow to come to you as well; let the space between you shrink until you are touching. Maybe at this time you are ready to fully embrace this story and take it into the heart of you. Maybe it will take many tellings before you are ready for that. Either way, as you touch, let a grand light begin to fill the room, a healing light whose source is your own Godself. Let the light fill and feed the room. Be bathed in the light, cleansed and quenched. Let this continue as long as you need or want.

As the light softens and fades, and with the knowing that came from this long-lost part of you, realize that this room hides a great gift. Under the bed, on a shelf, in a drawer, you know where to find it. This box may look like a pirate's chest or a jewelry case or a cigar box. Have a seat and open the box. What is the gift that your shadow gives you?

Think about what you will do with this item. Will you take it away? Leave it here? Or somewhere between these two? Maybe you can plant it in the garden back at the Sanctuary and see what grows.

Now it's time to go. Know that you can return to the Shadow House at any time.

As you leave the room, notice whether there have been any changes to the space. As you walk through the rest of the Shadow House, do you notice anything different?

When you go out the front door, you may wish to use the key to lock it behind you as an extra assurance that none go in or out without your consent.

Walk back to the edge of the clearing where the sphere of protection keeps the Shadow House safe and contained. Walk through the permeable barrier of the perimeter and then through the trees, along the path, back to your Sanctuary. Enter this holy place.

You may feel exhausted, or elated, or both. You may have conflicting emotions. Any of these are entirely apropos; all is perfect. Take a few moments with your ally to talk about your experience, receive their insights, or simply sit in silence and camaraderie.

If you've chosen to bring the gift back with you, place it on your altar, knowing that as long as it is here, it is never lost. If you'd like, take some time to plant it in the garden.

Now prepare to move back into the shared reality. Say goodbye to your ally and any others who may have helped you on your way. Bank the fire or put out the candles, whatever you need to do to prepare the Sanctuary for your leaving. Take a seat, and when you are ready, come back to the breath.

Take a breath in your sacred space, and breathe out. Breathe in and follow your breath into the darkness within you, and breathe out into the light. Breathe into your body and out, and breathe in and follow your breath back out into the room of light and noise, the shared reality. When you are ready, open your eyes and be here now.

Shadow House—Head, Heart, Hands
Head: What Scares You?

- Work on the questions from your travelogue pages, adding in these specific to the Shadow House:

  Did the House remind you of any place in the shared reality?

  What was the word over the door you chose to enter?

  What story did your shadow tell you?

  Was your ally present? How did they support you?

- Again, write for at least fifteen minutes, but more is better.

Heart: Whistling in the Dark

- The phrase "whistling in the dark" refers to a practice of acting as if one is braver than one feels. Find your whistling in the dark. Is it a song? A vision? A prayer? What never fails to give you courage?

Hands: Shadow House Model/Collage

- Create an image of your Shadow House using paper and pen, or boxes and glue, or images from magazines; alternately, create any physical expression of it, using your body to dance, or your voice to sing.

• Locate the House on your map.

The Gifts of Courage and Compassion

In the Shadow House, you gain many valuable experiences. Facing and embracing your shadows teaches you to forgive yourself and others, to revise your understanding of long-ago events, and to express yourself more freely. The influx of energy to your daily life can be deeply felt as you release those tight bonds of fear and pain. You become whole.

You are also reminded in the House of the importance of courage and compassion on this path: courage to seek out your broken pieces and compassion to accept them without judgment. You can practice these virtues and bring them more strongly into all parts of your life.

Your courage may be just a tiny ember when you begin. That's fine. It is perfectly appropriate to start small. You can lean on your allies, guides, and guardians. You can borrow their courage while you wait for yours to grow. You can use your strong will to push yourself into action, even when your knees are shaking. Will is the active aspect of courage, and they feed each other.

Even if you feel weak and scared much of the time, this doesn't mean that you aren't courageous! Remember the quote from Ambrose Hollingsworth Redmoon: "Courage is not the absence of fear, but rather the judgment that something else is more important than fear." I take this to mean that even if you are the most frightened person in the world, if your sense of what is right directs you to action, then you are also supremely courageous. You find your courage by looking for what scares you and then engaging it with your will.

This looks different to each person. What is simple for you might be a nightmare for me. I have a real problem with talking on the phone. If

I make a call every day, I'm using my will to build courage. You might have a hard time dancing in front of other people. Taking a belly dance class will build courage. Taking time for the more difficult aspects of your spiritual practice definitely builds courage.

Doing things that are hard for you is important because we are making this world every day, by our action or inaction. It's hard to confront someone about their racist remarks, but it has to happen. It's scary as hell to be on the front line of a protest and being yelled at or beat up by police. But someone has to do it. Putting oneself in harm's way to keep safe the land, water, and air that we all rely on to survive takes a special kind of courage. Those protectors have decided that the integrity of the earth is more important than their fear. Bless them.

I'm not saying that all these activities are suited for all people. Some people must make music and art and grow the food and feed the babies. But still, there may come a time when our courage is tested, and it is good to be ready.

You might need to start small. Baby steps are still steps! You might even need to begin with what SARK calls "micro-movements": tasks that can be completed in five seconds to five minutes—for instance, finding a pencil or putting a meditation pillow in front of your altar. Checking these tiny things off your list can give you a sense of moving forward, even if slowly.

The important thing, once again, is that you are standing in integrity and sovereignty over your life. If you make commitments and break them, or set intentions and don't follow through, you lose trust in yourself. Hello, shadow! If you back down from every argument because "it's fine," then you abandon yourself. Hello, shadow! It's a self-perpetuating cycle: when you act from fear, you call yourself a coward, and then you become convinced that since you are a coward, you can only act from fear. Hello, monstrous shadow of doom!

So, stand tall. Whether it's confronting someone on the bus about their abusive language or telling a partner that you're not happy, your truths deserve to be told. They must be allowed to breathe so they don't sink down into the darkness and become rooted as shadows. Accept that you are possibly going to look stupid, offend someone, make it worse, or be awkward. Also, you just might clear the air, unburden your Fetch, align with your Godself, save the world.

Seeking, Hearing, Speaking

One of the best ways to practice self-expression is to add this small prayer to your morning practice: I choose to seek, hear, and speak my thoughts and feelings today, however inappropriate they seem. (Note: "speak" doesn't necessarily mean "share with others.") After you say the prayer, follow through!

Keep a small notebook to write things down; use a pen with no ink if you're worried someone might find it. You're not necessarily creating a record, just letting things out of you.

Another good idea is to talk to a tree. They are often very good listeners.

Do try to make a commitment to visit the Shadow House regularly, perhaps at the dark of the moon. This will be an ongoing practice, as new shadows are constantly being generated. Go to your calendar now and fill in a date for yourself. Then treat the time as sacred. And always remember to begin and end in your Sanctuary and treat yourself kindly when you are in the thick of it. Remember to not only face toward the shadows but also turn toward the light and bask in its illumination.

Now, let's talk some more about compassion.

Courage inspires and is inspired by compassion. Compassion is a deep understanding of another's (or another part of our own) pain, accompanied by the desire to end the suffering. It takes courage to be truly compassionate, because we are open and vulnerable. This can be expressed in many ways.

Compassion is the outstretched hand offering money, clothing, or food. It's the listening ear and sympathetic hug. It's the heartfelt prayer that someone be healed.

Also, it's the aggressive encouragement to "get your butt back on the horse!" or "quit whining about your troubles!" True compassion may look like a charitable donation, or a "there, there, dear," but it doesn't always appear kind. Sometimes it looks like not being of immediate service; it looks like holding someone accountable, even letting them fail. Ending suffering is not the same as coddling weakness.

Ending suffering in the long term means that people should be at the center of their own problem-solving, and for you to help effectively, you have to trust that those in the center are strong enough to handle their part of the bargain. You have to trust that they can hold their own.

In the shared reality, this looks like believing that when your partner says they are happy to do the dishes, they really are, rather than second-guessing them. It looks like allowing your boss to ask for what they need, rather than running yourself ragged trying to do everything they might want. It looks like letting your children risk failing the test that they chose not to study for.

On the other hand, compassion is kind and intensely giving and forgiving. It requires that you care for those who truly cannot do something for themselves, delivering lunches to shut-ins or donating to relief efforts. It means knocking on the door when you hear your neighbors fighting rather than automatically calling the police. You can see how courage and compassion are related in these instances.

Sometimes it's hard to know what to do. There are pitfalls on either side of the path. You may find yourself in selfishness that looks like helping, or practicing tough love that isn't loving at all. Chögyam Trungpa Rinpoche calls this "idiot compassion," and it often shows up as an emotional overreaction to others' suffering, drawing attention to yourself rather than those in harm's way. Or it may mean the sort of giving that comes from an inability to say no. When you hear of a problem and, rather than taking the time to really understand it, you just jump in with your own solutions, you are acting from idiot compassion.

Sometimes we all need to call ourselves on our own behaviors while at the same time remembering our singular perfection as an imperfect being. (Pro tip: when you feel too beaten down, a visit to the Sanctuary is indicated!)

When you act in spite of fear, you gain courage. When you listen to yourself and others without judgment, you gain compassion.

Overcoming inertia, fear, and awkwardness is good exercise and helps you to move toward a world of honor, right use of power, and integrity. Your truest gifts require the ability to face whatever you must face to bring them forth.

The Shadows of the World

There are your own shadows and then there are shadows of the whole wide world. There are times when the tide rises, and you can see troubles begin everywhere, like a chain reaction of bad behavior. Sometimes you might meet one of these monstrosities when you are traveling in the secret country. What to do about them?

Remember that self-care is crucial. Keep yourself safe. Then, remember that you are not the only person in the world. Treat yourself well, with kindness and dignity, and also treat others that way. Being centered in your own strength and beauty is important, but it's not the only thing to consider.

All the people on the earth, human and otherwise, are here for some reason. We may have no idea what that reason is, especially when it appears that someone's influence is largely hurtful. As I'm writing this, there is terrible unrest in the world—wars, revolutions, and revelations of some very ugly sides of humanity. There's an upwelling of distrust, fear, and misplaced rage. I don't believe that this is some sort of test that humanity must pass, but I'm sure there's plenty we can learn from it.

These bursts of bad actions are like a large and scary shadow that we all share. What can one little person do about all that?

In the secret country, you can make a special trip to visit these shadows, but I encourage you to gather your allies first. Similar to what you'd do in the shared reality, if you were going to confront an unpredictable situation, it's important to know that you have some backup. Also, realize that what you find in your secret country is generated by you. It is a result of your possibly limited understanding of events and situations outside your immediate control. So, practice compassion as you hear the story of this shadow. Allow that it might be different from what you expect.

Or it might not. It might be just as you thought. You have a deep ideological difference with this entity. Though they have their own good reasons for believing as they do, you are simply not going to agree. And their beliefs present some sort of danger to you. You feel obliged to defend yourself.

Check in. Is this about you? Are you fighting someone else's battle? Are you doing that because they've asked you to or because you just can't help it? Or because you think the person whose fight it is just isn't strong enough on their own? In other words, are you disempowering someone by stepping between them and their own shadow?

Okay, it is about you. Is it possible to be respectful to someone you are about to fight? Of course. Run your Values Pentacle again and take your shield in hand. Allow it to gain a new power in this moment: the ability to dissipate shadows. Use it Captain America style and slice through and destroy the integrity of this worldly shadow.

And remember that what you're dealing with here is only your personal manifestation of this beast. If you want greater change in the shared reality, put out a call for others to help you with concrete actions to resolve these issues. When the problem is big, make the solution bigger.

And don't forget the immortal words of Wonder Woman: "We have a saying, my people. 'Don't kill if you can wound, don't wound if you can subdue, don't subdue if you can pacify, and don't raise your hand at all until you've first extended it.'"

World Shadows
Take some time to write about a troubling situation in the world. How might you participate in shifting that problem? Who might help you?

More Magick at the Shadow House

There are some spells that are particularly suited to the Shadow House work. Workings for protection, strength, mercy, and healing will support you in the challenge of unearthing your own darkness.

A Spell for Protection
This spell relies on creating a symbolic physical barrier in the shared reality as well as an energetic barrier in the secret country. You'll be focusing on empowering and protecting your best self.

HERE'S WHAT YOU NEED:

Salt (about ¼ cup)

Black pepper (a couple tablespoons)

An image of yourself that represents you at your very best (could be graduation day, wedding day, first day of citizenship, the day you passed the bar, your first sober anniversary, or even a baby picture if you feel that you want to go back to the beginning)

HERE'S WHAT YOU DO:

First, perform the Ha Prayer for Triple-Soul Alignment on page 28.

Next, do some sort of cleansing ritual, whether washing your hands with intention, or the full monty!

Mix the salt and pepper together, asking these two to protect you and keep away those who would harm you.

Breathe your way into your Sanctuary and, with your salt and pepper in hand, go outside and walk the perimeter of this holy place, sprinkling a strong line of protection around all that is most sacred to you. Remember that the Shadow House is the primary home of the shadows, but their effects may appear any place in the secret country.

When you've surrounded the Sanctuary with this protection, breathe your way back to the shared reality.

Now, put the image of yourself on a plate or a tray, something that's big enough that you can create that same barrier of salt and pepper around this aspect of you. Do that, again asking their spirits to keep you safe.

It is done.

A Talisman for Strength

For this working, you'll again be crafting something in the secret country and the shared reality.

HERE'S WHAT YOU NEED:

Any piece of jewelry that feels appropriate to you. This might be something you already own, or you could find a new one just for this. Depending on your relationship with your symbols, you might choose an OM, a hand of Fatima, or a cross. If you're not sure, use a pentacle to symbolize your Values Pentacle Shield. (Of course, if you're Pagan, the pentacle might mean any number of things to you. Do as you will.)

HERE'S WHAT YOU DO:

As always, do your Triple-Soul Alignment.

Also, as always, do your cleansing (just your hands or all of you).

Have your piece of jewelry in hand. Take some time to really look at it. Find what is beautiful about it, what feels powerful. Think about why you chose this piece. See if you can get a hint of the personality that is part of it. Do you feel a samurai warrior or ER doctor or blacksmith? What does strength mean to you, and what kind do you need?

Now, breathe your way into your Sanctuary. Find a comfortable place. Choose whether to invite this spirit into your sacred home, or if you'd prefer to meet them outside or somewhere else. Go to that place and call them. Tell them what you are looking for and ask for their assistance. If they are willing, then you are good to go. If they are not willing, it's time to start over!

Take some time with this helping spirit to charge your talisman. This might include blowing strong breaths of energy into it, or warming it between your hands, or passing it through a flame, or all of these.

Give gratitude to this new friend and return to your Sanctuary. Take a few moments here to just relax and feel the strength that already radiates from your talisman. Then return to the shared reality.

Now, whatever you did in the secret country to empower this tool, recreate it here if you can with air, fire, water, and/or earth.

Bone-Deep Healing

I mentioned before that shadow work can sometimes point out places that we thought were all healed up but turn out to be wrongly set or covering up another wound. This is a practice for easing the pain of those situations and allowing true healing to take root.

Begin in a comfortable place; lying down is great.

Breathe deep and let your breath be whatever it is in this moment. This is your own breath, your own rhythm, in your own time. Simply become aware of how the air feels in your nose and mouth. Become aware of how the air fills your lungs. As you breathe, let the breath you take in move into your center, the center of gravity, the center of your magick. Breathe it in and down to your feet. Relax. Breathe it down and into your ankles, calves, knees, thighs. Breathe down into your sex, into your glutes. Feel your legs relax. Breathe down into your back, into your belly, into your chest. Feel your torso relax. Breathe into your shoulders, your arms, wrists, hands, the spaces between your fingers. Relax. Breathe into your neck muscles, under your chin, your tongue. Breathe into your ears, behind your ears, the top of your head. Breathe into your skull. Relax.

Begin again with your feet, and this time move your attention through your body with an eye toward seeing tangles, knots, hurt and stuck places. Take your time and look deeply into your form. You are looking for places that might look okay at first glance but are actually needing attention.

See these places in your energy body and first, before anything else, tell yourself that it is okay to be exactly how you are in this moment. You can work for healing, but in this moment, it is okay to be hurt. Rest here. You might find yourself wanting to cry, and that's perfectly okay. Tears are often a sign that you are on the right track.

Now, remember how your Godself came into your Shadow House visit and gave you their blessing. See that same light coming into you now, beginning at your crown. Let that light fill you and feed you; let it move into all those broken and wrongly healed places in you, and see those spots softening. See them surrounded by the glorious glow of your Godself, and know that you are always loved and cherished by this most holy part of you.

Allow the strength and power of this light to move into the hurts and initiate healing. Some damage can be healed in moments, some takes years, but in this moment, you begin the healing that you choose.

Now, just for another minute, rest in this place of blessedness, of power and of love.

You can do this practice daily while you are working through the Shadow House material if you choose, or whenever you're having a hard time with life.

—— Seven ——

THE TEMPLE

Now you have dug deeply into the places of great light and great darkness. The core of you is stronger than it was, and you know yourself better.

It's time to turn toward a different, less personal experience of spirit. It is time to visit the home of Goddess or God or all the Gods or Spirit or All-That-Is.

It is true that everything is sacred. Every place and every power is holy. So, what is the Temple for?

In its simplest form, the Temple is Spirit's home in you.

Worshipping Your Gods

The Temple is the place in the secret country where you connect to something larger than yourself. You often find some sort of humanoid face on that larger something, which makes it easier to speak with, but it's not uncommon to meet deities that appear as a shaft of singing radiance, or a complicated mathematical shape, or an elephant. We are uniquely designed to be in relationship with all these things and can connect to light and idea and beast. This is the unique composition of humanity: we are one part animal, one part god, and one part the one who mediates these powers into the world of books and refrigerators.

There are, of course, many ways of experiencing deity in your life. For some, the gods are as real as we are, with fully developed personalities and desires and wills of their own. For others, there is one overarching god-being that encompasses all of life and everything in it, and it is differentiated only for the purpose of learning and experiencing newness. For still others, nature gives the sense of beauty and awe that one might otherwise seek from a supernatural source. Any or all of these may be true for you.

And there are different ways of connecting to the divine. Some consider the gods to have a higher standing than we human creatures, and they submit to the will of their deities and serve them devotedly. Others see their relationship with deity as a partnership, where each brings something of value to the table. Some simply desire friendship and inspiration from their spirits, and they're less concerned with defining the relationship.

You may come to the Temple with a strong idea of who your deities are, what they want, and what you want from them. Or you may enter with no expectation at all. At the least, I encourage you to approach with an open mind.

This can be complicated. Do you have a childhood history with gods or goddesses? Maybe the big kindly one with the long white beard, or the jealous one who condones rape and murder? Possibly the fecund earth mother or the blessed virgin? Did they feed you well? Did you ever feel threatened by them; e.g., were you told that you'd go to hell if you smoke, drink, have sex? Alternatively, what sort of reward were you promised if you kept to the obligations of the faith? How do you feel about that god and those activities now?

If you were indoctrinated into your religion by your parents, you might have chosen to leave your family's god as a part of a rebellion against authority. Have you ever cut god out of your life and then realized that you missed them? Have you been able to reconnect? If you were not raised in a religious household, do you feel that you lost out on something important?

In the Temple in the secret country, you can create your own pantheon. Who is the goddess who holds your hand when you are grieving? Who shares your celebration when good things happen? What god do you hope to make proud of you? If the deities you know, or know of, aren't fitting well in your life, you may want to seek new ones.

If you don't believe in a traditional idea of gods, then what might be a Temple for you? Maybe your place of practice looks like the most comfortable yoga studio or meditation hall filled to the brim with silence. Possibly, your Temple looks like a laboratory, and scientists are the clergy.

Sometimes you only find out what you deify when you look deeply at your own life and actions. What else might be considered so sacred to you that it becomes a guiding principle? Is your Temple a gymnasium where you worship the gods of fitness? A recording studio where you meet with the spirits of song? The trading floor of the stock exchange where you connect with deities of wealth?

Maybe you are most familiar with what have been called *small gods* of this tree, that bit of stream, or this farm. Those deities aren't big and extravagant, and sometimes they don't even have names. Instead, they are sort of a coalescence of the energy of a specific place or thing. These are some of my most precious relationships with spirit, and they hold the most intimate magick. When I eat the potatoes grown here on our farm, I am nourished by the gods of the spring water and the compost. When I put a fence around the oaks to keep the goats from eating the young leaves, I do so with respect for all the creatures that will be affected. The goat gods are not amused, but the oak spirits are grateful! I mentioned before that I'm a Dirt-Witch, and it follows that most of my deity interactions are quite informal.

In some religions, confession of one's wrongdoing (defined as not living up to the tenets of the faith) is an important part of the relationship with spirit. A while back, we talked about staying clear and clean with the Untangling Rite. These two things are closely connected! Even when you are not telling a spiritual counselor about your errors, you should be telling yourself. When you confess in the Temple, you may be admitting your transgressions to your gods, if they are interested in hearing them. It's also perfectly acceptable to tell your story to your own Godself. The important part is that you are offering yourself to the process of forgiving and being forgiven.

In the Shadow House, you may have met parts of you who were struggling with guilt and shame over their bad behaviors. When you listen to those stories, you are acting as the confessor for your own wounded parts. There is great healing power not only in speaking truth, but also in hearing it.

Is there any such thing as communion in your Temple? You might have something like the Christian concept of transubstantiation, in which you consume the body and blood of your god. Many Pagans consider that the harvest feast consists of their god's sacrifice for his people. Whether you consciously ingest the body of your god/dess in bread or meat or simply engage in prayer and meditation, you are communing with your god. If you are practicing sex magick, then you are communing with god on an entirely different level!

Your Thoughts on God

Spend some time thinking about how you want to connect with your gods. What do you want to give to them? What do you want from them? How can you create a more active relationship there?

Another aspect of the Temple is the Cemetery. Here are your ancestors of blood and lineage. Here are your dead dreams and other things that have outlived their usefulness. The Cemetery is a good place to remember that everything that has gone before feeds what is to come.

Your kin who have passed through the veil may have gone on to other lives, but often their shades remain, and in your secret country, this is what you are engaging with. Your memories of them will spark the connection, but you can also go beyond that simple story by inviting them to meet with you at the Cemetery, or another location in this holy place. Sit with them. Share tea (or whiskey) and cakes (or cigars). Enjoy each other's company.

Everything ends, eventually. Our human bodies, we know, will pass away. This is one thing that is true for everyone on the planet! But there are many other endings. A relationship, a job, a home—all feel right for a time, then no more. You might mourn the passing of your innocence in a literal or figurative sense. Losing the blinders of your ignorance about social and environmental injustice is life-changing for you and the world.

The Compost of Your Past
Think about a death you've experienced, whether of a person or a situation, that gave rise to a beautiful gift. Perhaps getting fired from a job opened the way to your dream career, or the ending of a love relationship put you into a deep state of self-reflection that's changed all your relationships since. What is the gift in death?

Many of us in the neo-pagan movement are trying to create a new religious reality. We don't believe in what we were taught by our parents, but we haven't quite got all the parts in place for our own belief system. The hyperrational aspect of our times means that talking about any real experience of spirit is awkward, if not entirely off-putting. Who tells the carpool driver that god gave them advice that morning? It smacks of evangelism: "I was on the phone with god and he told me that he would take me away to heaven if we don't give as much money as we can right now…" Also, we've been taught that religion is one of only two things one should never discuss in polite company—that and politics.

But if we never talk about our spiritual experiences, we continue to be isolated from each other in the exact areas where we could most benefit from being more connected. Truly, we all want to love and be loved, to be part of something larger than ourselves, whatever name we use for that something. Even atheists usually honor the cosmos in some way and see the beauty and intricacy of nature's creation. So I encourage you to stay connected to your spiritual community, online or in person. Speak what is true for you, but recognize that everyone has their own truth that is valid for them. Remember that the gods don't belong to any one person or group of people. Question whether you really need to agree on the details. You probably have much more in common than you think.

I do want to put in a word here about cultural appropriation. We've talked before about how your inner experience is not always reflected in the shared reality, and that's as it should be. But if you have an interaction in your secret country with a deity that clearly comes from a different culture than your own, it's a great opportunity to practice being quiet and learning. For instance, if a goddess who looks like Kali shows up in your Temple and you spend many difficult and profoundly moving hours in her company, that doesn't necessarily mean that you *know* the Kali, who is a central figure of Hinduism. Maybe she is the same, but maybe not. So it's best not to paint yourself as an expert; better to make a connection with someone who is a part of Hindu culture and see what else there is for you to learn about. Your unique relationship with this spirit may change or remain the same after your investigations.

Visiting the Temple

This is where you come to completely settle into meditation or exultation. There is no other priority here than connection with who or what lies beyond your usual reach. It is also a place to connect with others in spiritual practice. You might hold services, meetings, or shared meditations. (This makes an interesting astral travel or shared dreaming material for a group.) If you already have an existing practice with your gods, you will have your own terms and conditions with them that should be respected here. Consider the Temple work as an adjunct to your own customs.

Go to your altar in the shared reality and begin with the breath. Let the breath you take in fill you and feed you. Let the breath you take in invigorate the cells of you, and between the cells, the emptiness that is you. Breathe into your center, into that still point within you, that place of restful, peaceful calm. Breathe into that place and let it expand around your consciousness. As always, start in your Sanctuary.

Let an image begin to form around you of your most precious home in the secret country of yourself. Rest easy for several moments here. Do a Ha Prayer with the intention of aligning your souls and inviting Godself to be fully present on this journey. It is good to have the god that is you connecting to any other gods you might meet.

Now declare your intention: I go to the Temple to connect with Spirit and spirits, to learn the lessons of guidance and discernment. May I be blessed in this undertaking.

Rise from your comfortable place and go to the door. You know the way. Follow the trail that calls to you.

What does this path look like? Is it well tended or overgrown? Does it pass through the woods or across the meadow?

Notice how your feet connect with the earth as you walk. Swing your arms and feel the air moving against your skin. Listen for any insects or birds or other creatures accompanying you. Nod a respectful greeting.

When you see the Temple ahead of you, stop for a moment and take it in. Pay attention to how your heart feels in this moment. Apprehensive? Full of longing?

What do you notice first about this place? Does it seem neglected? Opulent? Sometimes folks spend all their resources on building and maintaining their Temple. Is that true for you?

What is the building made of? Stone, wood, adobe? Or maybe this is a large tent, like for a revival. Are there doors? Any windows? Do you see any light inside?

Maybe there is no building at all but simply a grove tucked away around a bend in the path. If this is true for you, what sort of trees are here? Maple, apple, manzanita?

Walk the grounds for a bit. Find the Cemetery and spend at least a few minutes here, looking at the memorials. Do you see any names you recognize? Anything that sparks your curiosity? Your ancestors of blood and lineage may be buried here.

Wander on. What else do you find? Is there a fellowship hall? Broad lawn, playground, community garden?

Now enter the Temple itself. What does it look like inside? A ring of simple wooden chairs around a bowl of water? A dirt floor with hundreds of burning candles lining the walls? Stained glass and soaring architecture? Is it larger inside than it appears from outside? Find a source of water, fill your cup, and drink.

Is there any music? Do you hear sweeping hymns or intense drum rhythms? Maybe melodic guitar picking or a cappella goddess chants? If there is no music and you would like some, bring it in to your sound and vision.

Do you find anyone here? A priestess in dark blue, kneeling before an altar or a priest smudging the room with Palo Santo smoke? Maybe one of your own gods is already here to meet with you.

Take a seat, in a pew or a chair or on the floor, as is appropriate. Close your eyes in your mind's eye. Breathe. Invite a vision of deity to come to you. Try not to be specific in your calling. Allow someone new to come to you, if you and they will it. You may meet an old god or a new goddess or someone you've never imagined.

Ask them what they love the most. Is this a god of wine, or books, or bards, or sickness, or death? A goddess of fear, or pain, or courage, or wild joyous laughter? A nonbinary deity of something that is only known to your secret heart?

Take at least five minutes to speak with this being. It is not advised to make commitments of any kind on this first foray. It's best to take time to clearly think over any agreements.

When you are finished with your conversation, be sure to give gratitude for this spirit's time and attention.

And prepare to depart from the Temple.

As you head back to your Sanctuary, check in with yourself. How do you feel now? Motivated? At peace?

When you get back to your sacred home, take some time to sit for a bit with your experience. If you have gathered anything on your trip, find a place for it here, now.

Take a seat when you are ready and come back to the breath.

Let the breath you take in fill you and feed you. Let the breath that you take in invigorate the cells of you. Follow your breath into your body ... and out. And in ... and out. And once more, follow your breath into your body and back out into the space of light and noise, the shared reality. And when you are ready, open your eyes and be here now.

Temple—Head, Heart, Hands
Head: Do You Believe in God?

- Work on the questions from your travelogue pages, adding in these specific to the Temple:

  What was your idea of the gods before your visit to the Temple?

  Has anything changed?

  What is your role in your relationship with the divine?

  What's the connection between your Godself and the gods you interact with?

- As always, write for at least fifteen minutes.

Heart: Praying to Small Gods

- Write prayers to your own small gods: the god of your spinning wheel, or a wine you adore, or the park you love best.

- Begin making your own prayer book. Collect prayers to inspire and comfort you, to give you courage and strength.

Hands: Temple Model/Collage

- Create an image of your Temple using paper and pen, boxes and glue, or images from magazines; alternately, create any physical expression of it using your body to dance or your voice to sing.

- Locate it on your map.

The Gifts of Guidance and Discernment

In the Temple, you receive guidance from spirit in many forms. You exercise discernment to improve your understanding of what you are told.

Guidance is not only heard in the secret country, though. It is a voice in the night, a spread of tarot cards, or a phone call at exactly the right moment. It's the song on the radio or the sudden rise of a memory, or a shift in understanding, like a key turning in a lock. You may look and look for it and not see it right in front of you. Or you may keep turning your head away only to have it pop up again and again until you are forced to acknowledge it.

Guidance is the universe talking to you.

God Herself speaks through everything. You might say that the entire cosmos is a conversation that Goddess Himself is having with all things. The word may look like a flower to you, but to me it looks like my grandmother saying hello. It may look to me like a bunch of lines carved on wood, but to you, the runes speak with clarity.

Guidance is that message told in words or feelings or images, which offers new information, turns you in a different direction, inspires you to great (or small) deeds. You receive guidance, sought or unsought, from the trees, the spirits, your own sweet souls. Guidance can be a gift when it helps you or a burden when it reveals to you what you'd rather not have known. Opening to the conversation that surrounds you expands your experience of the worlds and gives you access to new levels of potential. It's a good idea to learn all you can about the intuitions, nudges, and hunches that move you: What are they and where do they come from? How do you recognize "true" guidance amidst all the clamor of daily life?

A deep experience of any guidance begins with being open. A willingness to hear is the first requirement. If you are seeking information, it is important to acknowledge that you are asking for something. There's a humility piece here, a recognition that others may have something that would help you. At other times, you will have your own guidance to offer, your own hard-won wisdom that may really help someone else. Practicing being on both sides of this equation helps you to stay in balance, giving and taking as appropriate.

Learning the skill of listening is crucial: being silent while you wait for the message, reserving judgement until the message is delivered, being respectful and gracious with the messenger. Choose to practice active listening by restating what you thought you heard and asking for clarification. If you receive what looks like a clear reading about what job you should take, say, "Are you saying that … " and pull one more card or use a pendulum to get a yes or no answer. Only don't do this more than once or twice per question, or your cards might start giving you nonsense answers. No one likes it when their words aren't being heard!

Another key to opening to guidance is to choose the mode of listening by what type of message you seek in the secret country or in the shared reality. Listen in the garden to hear from the plants. Listen at your ancestor altar (or their home or grave) to hear your beloved dead. Listen while writing to capture Talker's thoughts. Listen in sitting practice to hear from Godself. Listen with runes or tarot or other revealed languages for spirit talk.

The language of guidance is up to the individual instance; you will create personal meanings for the events in your life. Often folks are gifted for a certain kind of guidance. Some of us hear voices or see visions. Some dream true. Others are gifted in seeking answers through languages others have developed; the tarot and the runes were given meaning many years ago by those who first received them.

Pro tip: you can establish your own guidance language by creating definitions for events, such as buying a lottery ticket whenever you see three crows on a wire. Notice how the universe speaks to you, specifically.

When the messages begin flowing in, you need to consider whether it is god or spirit or Godself really talking and not your immediate desire. How do you trust what you're hearing? Here's where the discernment comes in. In this case, judgment is good! It keeps you from acting out of your shadows.

The tools of discernment are many. First, there's your own good sense. Some messages feed so easily into your dysfunctions that you can see the problem right away. If you are constantly hearing bad things about people you don't like, you might consider the possibility that you are generating those messages yourself as a justification for your feelings.

Another good tool to check on your guidance is meditation: sitting or walking in silence for clarity. You can busy your Talker with a chant or a candle to gaze into, pray for Godself's assistance, and settle your internal chatter. At this point, it can be helpful to call in an ally to help you sort things out.

If you want your guidance to continue to make itself known, you need to pay attention. Imagine if a friend kept asking you for advice and ignoring it. Wouldn't that be a bore? All those who you might ask for information and insights deserve the respect of a thoughtful hearing. You may still choose not to act on what you're told, but courtesy is key!

Sometimes even with the help of your allies and guides, you can't get to the heart of a thing. In any case, it helps to work with a trusted friend, priest, or counselor in the shared reality. The key point when you are sharing your personal work with others is to be sure that these folks have your best interests at heart. You may find some folks are more interested in preserving the status quo than supporting your new exploration. Sometimes the closer you get to your biggest power, the more threatening you feel to others. Sometimes, they just fear losing you.

If you begin receiving messages calling you away from the clan, is there someone who will give you space for that questioning and at the same time challenge you when appropriate? Your guidance may lead you to experiences so new that your current life is left behind. How would you manage that? Who in your life can see you first as an individual, then as a member of their community?

It's important to note that these tools of judgment are ultimately wielded in the name of your personal code of ethics. If you receive a message that says, "Go ahead and take it," you have to consider this not only in the light of its authenticity as guidance, but also as an ethical question. Are you willing to do this? There may be times that the message is so clear that you consider something you never thought you would, to spark a change in your situation. You might find yourself in an unfamiliar position with regard to your beliefs.

This is a place of great potential and also great danger! When you are trying to figure out a long-standing conundrum, you need to get out of your normal ways. When you've already tried all the things you thought would work and they haven't, it stands to reason that you need to move out of your comfort zone and into your discomfort zone to really shift perspective. But when you are on unfamiliar ground, uncertainty can make you vulnerable. It is now that you stand on the work you've done in the

Sanctuary, and the Shadow House, with your values and your pentacle, and feel your strong center, your core truth, peaceful and sure. From that calm place, you choose a direction.

Your choice may not take you exactly where you thought you'd go or where you want to go, especially at first. You may find yourself in some dark bar late at night, figuratively or literally. Then comes another round of questioning: Are you scared for no reason, or is this actually a bad idea? Did that tarot reading really mean for you to leave your house at midnight and come to this hellish happy hour? Even if it did, are you ready for this? Do you want it? You'll be offered all sorts of challenges to help you get to a new place. Will you accept this one or wait for another? Which is the more empowered option?

Because guidance comes in arcane and symbolic language, it's often less than concise. Learning to interpret messages from cards or visions is an ongoing process. In some cases, you will never know with any surety what was meant by your guidance. Since it's pretty clear that life is always going to be uncertain, you have two choices: either fret about trying to make it more certain, or get better at living with uncertainty!

Trusting Your Intuition

Try taking an entire day and just allowing your intuition to be your guide. Do whatever you are drawn to do. This is especially fun and informative to do out in the world (away from the TV, computer, and phone, if possible!).

The Hall of Tarot

One of the most fruitful ways of receiving guidance is through the use of divination tools, such as the tarot or other oracular cards. In this practice, you go beyond developing a relationship with the spirit of your cards and begin working with the characters on the cards. Whether you are an experienced reader or you've never touched a deck in your life, this part of the secret country will enrich your divination skills. There is much to learn about yourself and magick in general by taking this arcane journey.

The defining characteristic of a tarot deck is the structure. There are always seventy-eight cards, broken down into the forty minor arcana, sixteen court cards, and the twenty-two major arcana. Sometimes the names of the cards are different, and often the images are, but there is a general flow that is common.

One way to think about it is that the minor arcana are the everyday folks doing everyday activities, the court cards are the ruling families of the various kingdoms, and the major arcana are the gods of the tarot universe. You can use this technique with any and all of these, but for now we'll begin with the majors, specifically the first three cards: the Fool, the Magician, and the High Priestess.

For this section, you will need a tarot deck. It can be fun to repeat these meditations with a variety of decks. You will have a different experience with each one.

The Arcane Journey

As with all your meditations, begin at your altar. Have your tarot deck at hand with the major arcana cards out and in order. We will begin with the Fool.

Breathe your way into your Sanctuary. Take a few moments to get centered and connected with your soul's home. You are going to be working with closed eyes and open eyes throughout this meditation. If you find yourself getting lost when you open your eyes, just close them again for a few moments and go back to your Sanctuary. You can take as long as you want to work through these cards. Usually three at a sitting is plenty!

Have the Fool card in your hand, the 0, what is before the beginning, the one who gave us the term "fool's leap" because of their trust that the universe will provide either wings or a valuable lesson! In your mind's eye, hold up the card before you. Recognize that you can step into the card, just like stepping through an open door. Do that now.

How does it feel? Nerve-wracking? Plain scary? Exhilarating?

Now, if you haven't yet, introduce yourself to the Fool. Spend a few minutes speaking with them about who they are and what they're doing. You might just stand there awkwardly for a few minutes. That's okay, too! You can always come back another time to make this connection.

When you're complete, thank the Fool and come back to your Sanctuary. If you've found anything, or if they've given you anything, find a place for it here.

And when you are ready, come back to your breath, open eyes, and return to the shared reality.

———————

As with your other journeys, do some writing on your experience. How did the Fool strike you? Charming? Alarming?

Did you get a sense of where the Fool might live, in relation to the other places on your map? Is there a "Fool's Home" somewhere? If so, locate it.

———————

Next, it's time to visit the Magician ...

Come back to your Sanctuary. Take a moment to rest and refresh.

Have the Magician card in your hand, card 1. The Magician is the first step into manifestation; he has received the tools of creation and is ready to make his mark on the world. In your mind's eye, hold the card before you. See it as a doorway and step through.

Meet the Magician in his own place. Introduce yourself. Ask him what he is working on and if he has any message for you.

When you are complete, thank the Magician and return to your Sanctuary.

Take a few moments to reorient yourself there. Set down anything you gathered on your trip. And when you are ready, come back to your breath, open your eyes, and return to the shared reality.

Do some writing. How was the Magician? Welcoming? Distant?

Can you find where you were on your map? Mark it if you can.

And the High Priestess…

Begin in the Sanctuary.

Have the High Priestess card in your hand, the second card of the tarot deck. She is mystery, the understanding that comes from inner wisdom. She holds occult knowledge and teaches you to trust your intuition.

Step into the card.

Take a moment to settle here and then introduce yourself. How does the High Priestess respond to you? Ask her for help with a puzzling issue.

When you are ready, thank the High Priestess and come back to your Sanctuary.

Take whatever time you need to settle, then come back to your breath. Open your eyes and return to the shared reality.

Again, writing!

Was the High Priestess able to help you with your quandary? What was her demeanor? Can you find her place on the map?

Try this with the rest of the major arcana, the minors, and the court cards. If you start at the beginning and work your way through the entire deck, you will have completed a very special secret country journey.

More Magick at the Temple

The Temple is an excellent place to work on issues that you'd like your gods to be directly involved in. Maybe these are problems that feel way too big for you to solve on your own, or maybe you just want to find another way to stay connected to your deities. Here are a few suggestions.

Cutting Ties Exercise

You are finally rid of a bad relationship, but the person continues to pop into your head in disconcerting ways. Make a special trip to the Temple. Ask your gods what you should do. Take some time to listen.

Go to a neutral location. The Temple has these safe places for us, a bench next to the wall or a table in the kitchen. Perhaps there is a special room just for these types of interactions. Invite your gods and allies to be with you for this conversation. Invite this person to come to where you are. Tell them, unequivocally, how you feel. Say all the words you couldn't say to their physical face. Finish the conversation in your most powerful way. Put them out and close the door behind. Lock it. It is done. (If you are being harassed in the shared reality, call a trusted friend, your mom, or the cops. Don't take a chance on your life.)

Most Powerful Allies

There may be times in your life when your gods want you to learn from someone else. I had this experience when a friend noticed that I had a bit of a whirlwind hanging around me, and he thought it might be one of the Orisha, who is associated with the storm, among other attributes. To sort this out, I met with another Orisha who I've worked with for many years, and she informed me that there were things she couldn't teach me, so I needed to go with my auntie for a bit to get some training. Thus began a very difficult but ultimately empowering few months!

If this happens to you, or if you're just interested in making new friends in the god realm, here's what you can do.

As usual, begin with breathing into your Sanctuary. Take a moment here and then head out to the Temple.

When you reach the grounds, call for your god or gods to be with you. If you have a deity practice already, you will likely have some sort of ritual around this. If not, just call to the god you met with last time you were at the Temple.

After they arrive, spend a little time chatting with them. Then ask that they introduce you to another deity or spirit that you are drawn to or that you feel is drawn to you. Remember that some deities have feuds with each other, so do a little research before you ask Hera to introduce you to Aphrodite.

When you've made a good connection with this new spirit, ask them what they have to teach you. Make plans, if you want, for some devotional work with them. Often deities will want some sort of effort on your part to maintain the relationship. If at any time you feel uncomfortable with what they are asking of you, call your own god or your own Godself back to strong presence. Be safe.

The Not-So-Silent Supper

This journey is particularly appropriate to the dark time of the year, between Samhain and Yule.

Begin with your breath. Allow the breath you take in to fill you and feed you. Allow your Sanctuary to arise around you, and after a moment to get your bearings, head to your Temple. Look for the kitchen or dining room; places for religious observation almost always have those! If you can't find it, call it forth by visualizing any place like that you've been.

Now enter the kitchen and find your beloved dead awaiting you, friends and family who've passed to another world. There may be tears. That's perfect.

Depending on how your family worked, you might all gather in the kitchen and cook together, or you might find all the food already prepared for you. Either way, adjourn to a long table with lovely place settings and candles. Take a seat.

This supper may include huge laughs, tears, even arguments. Remember that this is your personal reality and that you can shift it to your pleasure. Sometimes disagreements are necessary, but other times, it's better to just avoid certain subjects in this setting.

Take as much time as you like, partying with your dear departed ones. And when you are ready, bid them farewell. Return to your Sanctuary. If there's anything you gathered on this trip, find a place for it here. Maybe a flower from your grandmother or a piece of jewelry from your aunt.

THE SCHOOL

Eight

Now it's time to step away from these deep personal reflections and visit the place where you interact with all the intelligence that the worlds have on offer.

At the School, you learn about art and history, mathematics and poetry. You also learn about learning: how to find the information you seek, keep an open mind, and think along new lines. You are encouraged in your enthusiasm for fourteenth-century symphonies or modern dance, quantum physics or cake decorating. There is room for every fascination and curiosity.

All Knowledge, Some Wisdom

The School is the place in the secret country where matters of the mind are paramount. You learn, of course, from every interaction you have, but the School is meant for intensive research and experimentation. It is the most natural home of the scientist and the poet. In other words, your Talker.

Talker is filled with delight at the myriad educational opportunities here at the School. So much to learn and explore and add to your store of

133

knowledge! Maybe if you are lucky and integrate your learning well, that knowledge will become wisdom.

As we discussed way back in chapter 2, Talker is the *I* that you usually think of as your most vocal self. They're in charge of words and numbers and calendars. They are the part of you that calls a friend to plan for another friend's birthday party. Talker can handle a to-do list like nobody's business. (At least they have the potential to. Your mileage may vary. Mine certainly does.)

Your Talker is the one who decided to take this journey to the secret country, though they may have been influenced by your Fetch and Godself. They buy the materials and schedule the times of practice. They read these words and roll the ideas around to see how they look and feel from all sides. Talker's got smarts. And it's good to have smarts when you're going to School!

Talker is not infallible, though. One thing that can happen with them is an imbalance between intuition and logic. Remember, Talker rules both halves of the brain, and both are required for healthy functioning. The right brain, or creative side, is more personal; it might make less sense to others, but it has its own internal methodology and consistency. This part is more easily connected to Fetch, as they share an openness to spontaneous bursts of inspiration.

The left brain, or more objective side, is what allows you to participate in social situations. It understands at least the rudimentary rules of our society, and it allows you to interact with others in ways that are mutually beneficial. It's also good at math.

Talker is tricksy and gifted in making things up, to your benefit or your detriment. This creativity with words is what makes Talker an excellent storyteller, a talent that can be used for good or ill!

To create something that's never been seen before takes imagination, the ability to see what is not there, has never been there, but may be brought into being. This is one of the gifts of Talker: to dream a thing and then to make it. Your Talker is a visionary, taking information and experience and from it, calling forth a theorem, a poem, or a song.

Talker wants to learn, and here at the School, you will find your teachers, those wise guides who will challenge and inspire you. They can help you see what you already know and point you to questions that you might not have thought to ask. You will find the materials and the settings appropriate to your interest.

If you love books, go to the Library. All the books ever and never written are there. You can read and research to your heart's content. Find lost manuscripts, scrolls, or papyri.

If you are a painter, go and meet with the masters (or mistresses?) Take a lesson from Frida Kahlo or Salvador Dali. Get the secret of that amazing blue, or how the light comes in just so.

If you are a musician, visit the Music Department. Meet the spirit of your instrument there and let them show you exactly how they want to be played. There is a different kind of magick to be made between you and them in this place where you can speak on more intimate terms.

If you are a playwright or an actor, go to the Theater. Connect with the Bard (who was s/he really?). Watch the process from bare-boned story through set and setting, intonation, and movement.

Perhaps you want to perform experiments in the Chemistry Lab, or track the stars and planets at the Observatory; or you are a dancer, or a writer, or you would like to build any of these skills. All you could possibly wish to learn is taught at the School.

And who are the teachers? Are they spirits or gods or mysterious angels or aliens? All of these might be true. Or maybe they are energy patterns that have become egregores through continued attention (like the shade of Shakespeare, or the imprint of Einstein). They might even be expressions of your deeper self, your imaginative subconscious showing itself in a new way.

The School is a good place to get a reminder that all your learning is personal. There is an important component of knowledge that comes from within you and can't necessarily be explained by objective facts. Intuitive truth has validity; you can absolutely use your perceptions to guide your own life, and to create the world you desire, but you can't necessarily use those same guidelines for everyone.

To be clear, if you go into the Physics Lab here and Albert Einstein gives you some new insights on relativity, you still need to bring those ideas out into the shared reality and submit them to the usual scientific testing for them to be recognized as true for all. It's quite possible that the laws of nature operate differently in your secret country!

To truly get the most out of your experience in the School, it's best to maintain a commitment to the spirit of inquiry. Even when you think you see everything clearly, be willing to reconsider if new information presents itself.

There's a great story about three scientists traveling by train. They had just crossed the border into Scotland when the first looked out of the window and saw a single black sheep in the middle of a field. "All Scottish sheep are black," he said. "No, my friend," replied the second, "some Scottish sheep are black." At which point the third looked up from his paper and glanced out the window. After a few seconds' thought he said, "In Scotland, there exists at least one field in which there exists at least one sheep, at least one side of which is black."

Now, this is a funny story, but it speaks directly to how we translate experience into knowledge or wisdom. On one end of the spectrum is the assumption that if a thing is true in your eyes right now, it must be true for everyone always. This fundamentalist perspective is obviously flawed. On the other hand, we find the kind of overly accurate statement that doesn't allow for any assumptions at all, no matter how likely they are. The middle ground is a more comfortable place for most of us and gives the best balance between what we think we know and what we know we know.

A commitment to true wisdom means recognizing when you are full of malarkey and not being afraid to change your mind.

The School reminds you to never stop learning, to be willing to wear the mantle of student for your entire lifetime. Recognize that you are a teacher as well, however unskilled you think yourself to be. You know things that someone else doesn't know, and in the spirit of generosity, you may offer your knowledge to others. In this interplay of ideas, you find yourself engaging with new concepts, perhaps building on others' works and expanding them into your own life.

The exchange of knowledge is critical for a healthy community, internal or external. The worlds work best when everyone moves toward their own interest and builds their own understanding and skill. When all come together, each has something to offer because all have grown. This diversity of exploration is as important to our society as the diversity of genetics is to an ecosystem. Every one of us is necessary in ways that we may not ever understand, so go ahead and follow your interest, which just might turn out to be your bliss!

Sharing Knowledge and Power
Think about what you are really good at. Baking cookies? Internet research? Milking goats? Are there opportunities for you to share your skills with others? Can you create those opportunities?

Think about what you'd like to learn. To dance the tango? To speak French? To prune fruit trees? Do any of your acquaintances know how to do these things? Can they teach you?

Visiting the School
Go to your altar and begin with the breath. Let the breath you take in fill you and feed you. Let the breath you take in invigorate the cells of you, and between the cells, the emptiness that is you. Breathe into your center, into that still point

within you, that place of restful, peaceful calm. Breathe into that place and let it expand around your consciousness. As always, begin in your Sanctuary.

Let an image begin to form around you of your most precious home in the secret country of yourself. Rest easy for several moments here.

Do a Ha Prayer with the intention of aligning your souls and inviting your Talker to be fully present on this journey. Talker has the perfect brain to make your efforts here fruitful.

Now declare your intention: I go now to the School in the spirit of curiosity and open myself to new forms of creativity. May I be blessed in this undertaking.

Rise from your comfortable place. Is there a particular door that leads to the School? Open that door and step onto the path.

How do you think about going back to School? Do you have any memories of School coming up right now? The smell of pencils? The taste of paste? The color of the first metallic crayon you saw? Do you feel the anticipation of beginning a new course of study? Perhaps you had that feeling when you started the journey into the secret country of yourself. Perhaps you've been walking all this time with a sense of excitement and possibility.

Do you have any idea of where you'd like to go first? What are you most interested in studying? And with whom?

You don't need to bring anything with you on this first visit to the School, but you may feel more comfortable with a pencil box full of newly sharpened pencils or your laptop or tablet safely in its case. It's entirely up to you. Anything you find yourself needing, you can call to you in the moment.

Walk on until you find yourself at the edge of the grounds, with the whole campus laid out before you. See it in its entirety, like a great map. Is the School all in one building or spread out amongst many? Are there any buildings at all?

You might see a grand castle with students flying around on broomsticks, à la Harry Potter. Or maybe what you find is more like the Unseen University of Terry Pratchett's Discworld, and you're looking forward to meeting the orangutan librarian. For you, the School might appear as a set of canvas tents or other movable huts so the teachers may travel easily from place to place. Maybe the classrooms are treehouses or caves.

What were you expecting? Are you surprised? Is there anything missing? Maybe it's up to you to create exactly what you're seeking.

Wander around a bit. Let your curiosity be your guide. Peek into classrooms. Sit under a tree. Find a drinking fountain or other source of water. Fill your cup and drink.

Have you gotten any sense of what you are here to learn? Do you have an idea of who you'd like to find to be your teacher?

If not, that's fine. You can take your time. If you choose to, you can say, "I am ready to be taught what I need to know."

Does anyone appear when you say that? If not, that's okay. It might just be time for you to be your own teacher for a while.

Wander on until you find the Library and step inside. How is the light here? Is the Librarian present? Is there a specific book you'd like to find? Ask for help with that. Figure out what the borrowing situation is here. Can you take a book with you back to your Sanctuary? You make the rules here, by whatever measure you choose. Spend as much time here as you'd like before, again, letting your feet find their own way out of this place and on to the next.

Go now to the department you'd most like to visit. Do you want to see the dance, music, or art studios? Or are you more inclined toward the labs: physics, chemistry, or engineering? Again, put out the call to the teacher that you'd like to help you learn more about any of these subjects. Maybe it is the spirit of mathematics itself that teaches you. Or the muse of poetry. Here, as you know, you choose your own educational adventure!

Spend at least five minutes in your favorite classroom, whatever form that takes.

And now it's time for a break from this learning. Bid farewell to any beings that you've been with here and head back to your Sanctuary.

Take a moment to sit with your experience. If you have gathered anything on your trip, find a place for it here, now.

Take a seat when you are ready, and come back to the breath.

Let the breath you take in fill you and feed you. Let the breath that you take in invigorate the cells of you and between the cells of you. Follow your breath into your body ... and out. And in ... and out. And once more, follow your breath into your body and back out into the space of light and noise, the shared reality. And when you are ready, open your eyes and be here now.

School—Head, Heart, Hands
Head: Filling the Library with Books

- Work on the questions from your travelogue pages, adding in these specific to the School:

  Were there any other students there?

  What sort of classes did you see being offered?

  Did any teacher appear to you?

  What department did you find yourself drawn to?

  Make a list of never-written books you'd like to find in the Library.

- Again, write for at least fifteen minutes!

Heart: You're Wrong! Isn't that Awesome?

- Practice saying, "Oh, I must have made a mistake." Begin sentences with, "In my experience ... "

- Recognize that one aspect of learning is discipline. Is there anything you want to practice and get really good at?

Hands: School Model/Collage

- Create an image of your School using paper and pen, or boxes and glue, or images from magazines; alternately, create any physical expression of it, using your body to dance or your voice to sing.

• Locate it on your map.

The Gifts of Curiosity and Creativity

At the School, you can learn so much about yourself, your desires, your passions. Two virtues that support those explorations are curiosity and creativity.

In this context, curiosity means a lively interest in people, places, and things. It means never entirely believing that you know all the answers. It's the unending search for truth (which is unending because you can't possibly know all there is to know!). It has an objectivity, a lack of attachment to one's own opinion. Curiosity keeps you looking with interest, but without assumption. It means maybe not being right. Also, other folks maybe not being wrong. It means respecting all possibilities as being, well … possible, within reason.

You may have heard that curiosity killed the cat, but did you know that satisfaction brought him back? Ha!

Curiosity is the hallmark of the scientific method that inspires the doctor to propose a theory, test it objectively, and prove themselves correct (or not). It's the lightly held ideas that the priest has about how a person can heal from trauma, the actions they need to take in the Otherworld, and wellness. One can feel very confident in their abilities and still be curious about what else is feasible.

Curiosity is a skill we all can build. A great exercise for doing that is challenging your own beliefs.

You hold within you many ideas that you take as fact. Everyone does. You may have heard the clever statement, "Don't believe everything you think!" It sounds glib, but this is a powerful concept. If we can disengage from our habitual mental processes, we open to different truths from others or from within ourselves.

There's a difference between thinking and having a thought. Thoughts are immediate and reactive, arising spontaneously out of a situation or process. Thinking moves and grows and becomes different; it's done a little work to get where it is.

Thoughts appear, flitting through your consciousness (or unconsciousness), then move on if you don't grab hold of them somehow. The difficulty comes when these unconscious, reactive thoughts create paths across the sky of your awareness so that you begin to expect them, count on them, create frameworks around them. It is these thoughts arising out of your beliefs that give the greatest freedom when questioned. This questioning doesn't mean that you must give those beliefs up. It just means that you are testing them against your previous experience or potential future experiences, to see if you want to keep them.

How do you do that?

The easiest way is to start with looking for things that have an emotional impact. Anger is usually an easy road to follow. Let's start with something that makes a lot of folks mad, including me! Let's start with traffic.

Perhaps, like some, you are impatient with slow drivers. You have a litany of mean prayers you recite when you're stuck behind someone not going the speed limit. It's intense and uncomfortable and you'd really like to change that.

Listen when you are in this situation to the story you're telling yourself. Maybe that story begins with how thoughtless they are, how inattentive and disrespectful, how they don't care about anyone but themselves. (How do I know about this mind-talk? You get one guess.)

Acknowledge that the story you're telling about this person was entirely created by you (or me). Sure, it's possible that they are just a bad driver or they're actively trying to make you mad, but it's more likely that they are coming home with a new baby, they are just learning, or they simply feel safer at 35 mph. Perhaps they are struggling with a weighty problem; maybe their child or their parent is ill. There are so many reasons why a person might drive slowly or distractedly. When you assume that you know someone's motivations, well, you know how that goes. If you consider that this might be happening because this person is having a hard time right now, you can be compassionate to their plight instead of judging their behavior. You can release their hold on your mental and emotional processes.

That's a good first step, but there is even greater richness waiting for further digging. The question of what this anger means has yet to be answered.

Replay that mind-talk. What were the assumptions about the driver? That they were disrespectful, unaware, thoughtless. The anger that's attached to those ideas is strong and points to a belief that these are bad or negative qualities. Think about that.

Disrespect is bad. Is this always true? In the realm of civil disobedience, acts can be disrespectful to an outside authority but fully respectful of one's own authority. Can you accept that sometimes disrespect to others has a worthy place in one's repertoire, even that it is crucial?

Lack of awareness is bad. Is this always true? Awareness is important in the sense that you have an expanded viewpoint from which to form your opinions, but do you have to know everything about what everyone thinks or does? Is attention to every possible point of input desirable or even possible? Not likely.

Perhaps this person is purposefully listening to what their Godself is telling them is safe. They may be disrespecting the law, or our need to get somewhere quickly, but it's hard to argue with someone fully in their power traveling at their own speed. Your assumptions and attendant anger are not affecting them at all. It's all up to you to carry the burden of frustration or set it down. And by the way, anger and resentments make excellent fodder for the Untangling cup!

This is a pretty easy example, though, having to do with strangers on the road. Sometimes the situation is much closer to home.

Sometimes you will put your opinion to the test and find out that, indeed, someone is being hateful and hurtful, and whatever their reasoning, you don't need to put up with their behavior. You can remove yourself from their presence or vice versa.

Please don't go to extremes with questioning yourself. This practice is designed to help you find clarity, not allow you to remain a victim. Trying too hard to find sympathy within you for an abuser is not helpful for you or them. If you are ever confused about this, a visit to the Shadow House (or a priest or therapist) can be helpful. The lessons of courage and compassion continue to arise!

Thoughts vs. Thinking

Take some time to sit with a situation that makes you upset or angry. Apply these principles to that state of affairs. What do you come up with?

Now, let's talk about creativity.

Think about the intersection of creativity and curiosity: not all that long ago, humans were earthbound. Then a lot of clever folks said, "What if?" They made plans, built machines, wrecked them, built new ones. Now humans can fly, glide, hover. What's next?

The world is inherently creative. It's also destructive, but even that is its own sort of creation. The boiling away of water creates steam that can be used to power a machine. The knocking down of the barn creates scrap wood that can be used to lay a floor.

Creativity means thinking outside of normal conventions. It happens in the lab, the studio, the backyard, the forest. It can be huge, like building a twenty-story wooden man with the express purpose of burning it down, or tiny, like stem cell research. It can be simple, like making up new recipes to feed your family or choosing to dress all in vintage clothing, or complicated, like designing a new kind of prosthetic limb that responds to electrical pulses from the brain. All of these are outpourings of originality.

Creative expression is of paramount importance to the whole secret country journey. At this point you may have already done many of the exercises from the "Head, Heart, Hands" sections of the previous chapters. What have you noticed about that process? Did you find it confusing? Difficult? Fun? Exciting? Are you judging yourself for your lack of talent or admiring your growing skills?

Creativity is not always easy. In fact, it's often arduous. By definition it includes experimentation, which very occasionally results in a masterpiece, but other times just makes an unholy mess! In which case, if it is your intention to come up with a final product, it's back to the drawing board. New lessons learned!

You will get stuck. Creativity is not only about the burst of inspiration that makes everything feel effortless. At times it will be difficult to keep going. You will feel clumsy, slow, stupid. That's fine. Just keep going! Get okay with a lack of grace. That is part of the process.

Sometimes what you need to help your creativity along is to take up a new tool. If you are stuck in painting, try singing. If you get writer's block, try coloring for a while. If you feel like you have no talents at all, I promise you you're wrong. I encourage you to consider all the things you do as an opportunity to experiment, to free up that juice that will help you think in new ways.

There are many ways to purposefully expand your creativity. A good beginning is to break routines wherever you find them. If you think about it in terms of just trying something new, there are infinite opportunities to make it happen. Start small. Drive home by a different route. Eat breakfast for dinner. Offer yourself new experiences. Whether you enjoy them or not, you are loosening up the constraints on your brain, filling in the rut you get stuck in.

Another helpful option is to allow yourself to get bored. Put away the phone, computer, tablet, and just sit. First, you'll get restless. Then tired. Then you just might find that your brain can't stand it anymore and it wanders off in a new direction!

Julia Cameron, in her book *The Artists' Way*, suggests doing "Morning Pages," three uninterrupted pages of (longhand) writing each morning before anything else. Writing in the morning gives you time before your internal critic wakes up. If you commit to this practice and really do it each day, you will find that not only is your creativity strengthened, but also your willpower!

Give yourself permission to be weird. It can be intimidating to stand out in a crowd, but oh, how delicious to fully express the real you! Take another look at all those people who seem *so normal*. When you only meet others in serious public places like work or the PTA meeting, everyone is on their best, most socially acceptable behavior. Recognize that lots of those folks are letting their freak flag fly in other settings, from worshipping strange gods to knowing all the words to every Disney song to dancing around naked in their living room.

Please, do let your creativity flow! The world needs more weirdos, those who pay attention to the lightning bolt of inspiration and keep alive the coals of the work it takes to bring visions into the shared reality. The more you open to your creative impulses, the more you become all the best of what humans can be.

The Library

The Library is one of my personal favorite places in any reality! I spent much of my childhood between the pages of this book or that. I would stay all day and night in Middle-earth or Narnia or on Perelandra if I could. Those places felt welcoming to me in a way that the shared reality often didn't.

Perhaps you are a bookish person as well. If you are, I bet you also have spent many happy hours putting yourself into the stories you read, fighting the great Dragon King or becoming friends with him; stealing the sacred golden cup, or returning it to its rightful owner; marrying the prince or princess or beast or god. What a gift is a well-told story!

Even if you are not enamored of books, there is much to gain from your time in the Library. Some tales are found between pages, but others are told by the ancient voices of master tellers. Either way, by your listening, you can try on different ways of being.

Sometimes when you hear a story of violence or heroism, you might think, "Oh, I could never do that!" But part of the magick of the story is that you get to, without repercussion, consider the possibility that you really could do that, either hide the body or save the child. The circumstances of each person's life lead them to choices that make sense in that situation, whether the rest of us approve or not. We are all both more noble and more ridiculous than we think we are at different times. In the arms of a story, you can consider why a person would do a thing, what could motivate them, and what could motivate you. And in the depths of another's experience, you learn about yourself.

Carl Sagan said this about libraries in his book *Cosmos*: "The library connects us with the insight and knowledge, painfully extracted from Nature, of the greatest minds that ever were, with the best teachers, drawn from the entire planet and from all our history, to instruct us without tiring, and to inspire us to make our own contribution to the collective knowledge of the human species."

Mowgli and Cerridwen

Let's go now to that Library and see what tales you might learn from.

Go to your altar. Breathe yourself into your Sanctuary. Take a moment to get situated.

Make your way to the School and from there to the Library. See this glorious home of thoughts and visions recorded for your edification and pleasure.

Wander the stacks for a bit until you find the fiction section. Go to the K's and find Kipling, Rudyard, *and* The Jungle Book*. This is a collection of tales that mostly take place in the jungles of India, the first few of which describe the life of Mowgli, a boy raised by wolves; taught the ways of the jungle by the great brown bear Baloo, and protected by Bagheera, a sleek black panther.*

This story (and the others in The Jungle Book*) have been made into several movies which vary in their adherence to the source material. Feel free to play among any of those that you enjoy, but we start here with the original writings.*

Open the book and read these words:

Now Rann the Kite brings home the night
    That Mang the Bat sets free—
    The herds are shut in byre and hut,
    For loosed till dawn are we.
    This is the hour of pride and power,
    Talon and tush and claw.
    Oh, hear the call! —Good hunting all
    That keep the Jungle Law!

Read some more, if you like, in or out of the shared reality. You might want to go back and forth for a bit if you are using the physical book.

The story begins with the lame tiger Shere Khan attacking a woodcutter's family around their campfire. In the confusion, the baby is separated from his parents, who leave thinking that their boy's been killed. Shere Khan is slowed by his infirmity, compounded by the fact that he burned his feet in the flames. This gives the toddler time to make his way through the jungle to a cave where Mother and Father Wolf are just awakening for the hunting time at dusk.

Take a moment now to feel the jungle rise up around you. Feel the humidity in the air, smell the thick pungency of the undergrowth, see the thick trunks of the trees. Feel the strength of your muscles, your lithe body made for this predation. Feel too the hunger roiling in your belly, the anger at having missed your kill, the pain of your blistered feet. There is no time to rest, though; you must find food soon, and the man-cub seems the likeliest prey.

Shere Khan comes to the wolves' cave but is unable to fit through the small entrance hole. He is frustrated and furious and demands they turn over the child. Mother and Father Wolf are having none of it. Mother stares down the tiger and says, "And it is I, Raksha [the Demon], who answers. The man's cub is mine, Lungri—mine to me! He shall not be killed. He shall live to run with the Pack and to hunt with the Pack; and in the end, look you, hunter of little naked cubs—frog-eater—fish-killer—he shall hunt thee! … Go!"

Now shift your perspective. Feel the lankiness of your long body, the brush of your tail, the warmth of the cave and your cubs. How fiercely you will protect them, including this new naked baby. Feel your legs stiffen and the curling back of your lip as you snarl at this threat to the safety of your family.

Shift perspective again. Feel the fear that you, as Father Wolf, have for your children. Mother is adamant that she will keep the boy, but two in the council must speak for him, who aren't his parents. Will there be two who will take a chance on this strange creature? There is no way to tell. But still it must be done. Feel your determination to press your case and your resolve to abide by the decision of the pack.

At the meeting, it appears that none will stand for the boy, until Baloo offers his support and Bagheera offers two freshly killed bulls as payment to the pack to let the boy stay. Time passes.

And now you are the man-cub, Mowgli. Feel the strength of your gangly arms and legs and the great freedom of having no other concern than food. See yourself climbing up a tree toward Bagheera's voice calling "Come along, Little Brother!" When you reach the place where he rests, climb up on his back and lie down along his length. Feel the softness of his fur against you and the vibration of his purr. This is the pure sensual pleasure of two animals enjoying each other's warmth. Relax.

Of course, Mowgli's story goes on and on, and there are many other adventures that can be told! Go further into the tale, if you wish, in whatever form you like: the tiger, the wolves, the boy. Or explore what it is to be the bear, licking honey from your paws, or the panther, slinking through the trees, drinking from the river.

When you are ready, close the book and find yourself back in the Library.

If you choose to, you may leave now and go back to the Sanctuary, and from there out to the shared reality. Or you might wander the stacks for a bit first.

The above story was relatively modern, but there is much to be gained by exploring the older mythologies as well. They don't always show up in book form, and even when they do, we know that these legends were told over and over for many years by many tellers and may have changed dramatically over time. You can also put your own stamp on the old tales, bringing them into a modern understanding or putting a different spin on who the villains and the heroes might be.

Here we look at a new version of an old myth about the goddess Cerridwen. Usually this story is told with the goddess as a vengeful mother who truly wants to kill the boy who stole the potion that she had meant for her own son. I have been led to tell it a bit differently. In my version, the Lady is a teacher and the boy her apprentice, though he doesn't realize it at first.

This is also an example of sticking with one character's point of view throughout a story and digging deeper into their individual journey.

Breathe your way to your Sanctuary. Sit for a moment there. From there to the School, and then the Library. Make yourself comfortable.

Then, in your mind's eye, close your eyes. Listen.

In this story, you are a child: not much use to anyone, a daydreamy kid. Maybe your visions are larger than what this place can offer you, this place where you've grown up. Maybe you feel constrained, contained by the circumstances of your life. Take a moment to feel that sense of being limited by your circumstances. Feel that desire for something more burning within you.

There you are wandering through your days, and the goddess Cerridwen, comes to you and says, "I want you to work for me. It's a simple task, but not an easy one. You must be willing to give up entirely a year and a day of your life in service to me. Will you commit?"

How do you answer? Are you willing to give up all the life you've had, for the chance to become something more?

Let's presume that you are, for the sake of the story. Cerridwen brings you to her dwelling. What does this place look like?

She brings you to an immense cauldron and says, "I will be filling this big pot with a wondrous, amazing, incredible spell that will bestow the gifts of magick, poetry, and wisdom. Your charge is to stir the pot."

You take your place there. There is a blind fire tender there as well, feeding wood to the fire beneath the pot, but he is not your concern. It is for you only to stir and stir steadily without fail. The next day, the Lady comes and she drops a wildflower into the pot and she says, "This is the alpine daisy. The property of the alpine daisy is to invigorate the inner senses," and as she drops the flower in you stir. And you stir. The next day, the Lady brings a smooth stone and she drops the stone into the pot, and as she drops it, she says, "Here is a river stone. The stone understands when to be still and when to be moved." And you stir. The next day, the Lady comes and she sings a song of the sun and the stars in the heavens. She sings into the pot and you stir. It's hypnotic, this movement, around and around.

Each day Cerridwen comes, and each day she puts a flower or a stone or a song into the pot, and as you listen to her words, her poetry and prose, you realize that something is starting to grow inside of you. Every day she holds her hands around the sides of the pot and she chants the song of making. She chants the names and the potentials of the stars, and she chants the names and the properties of the plants and the stones. Every day that you are here, your knowledge is growing. She is putting books on the shelves of your mind, but you have no true understanding.

Time passes and the Lady sings the song of the seasons, and the seasons cycle around you, appearing and disappearing in their own time. The heavens turn above you, and the Lady's song informs every moment. And information gathers in your mind.

Then one day the Lady comes and she looks you unblinking in the eye and she says, "It is time. Tomorrow morning, the moon will set and the sun will rise and I will come. I will take the first three drops of this potion that has been so carefully crafted . . . " You feel she is telling you this for some reason, but you are not sure what that is.

That night, you watch the dew collect on the leaves as the full moon gives her blessing, and you wonder what tomorrow will bring: What will you do when you are free? And the morning comes. The bright sun rises and still you stir. And as you stir, you are thinking of where you will go and what you will eat and who you will dance with. And you are thinking of what it means that the stars have names and stories of their own, and stones are alive and plants can heal or harm. Your brain is alive with all these facts that have been poured into you over the past year. And then you hear a shout and you are startled, and you drop the stirring stick. The stick falls into the potion and splashes up and onto your hand, and right quick, you stick that hand in your mouth.

O-ho-ho! What is this? Coursing through your veins? Enlivening every molecule of you? Your mind flashes with thoughts, your hands are hot with energy, your heart begins to open, and you hear the Lady's voice ringing in your head: "I wondered if you would take this power. Now that you have, I must make sure you either grow into it or die by it. You cannot hold it without challenge. You cannot hold it without proving your worth. Expect change. Soon you will forget who you are and I will not remind you. I will try to kill you and you will seek to live. Simple."

There is no time to think! You take two steps, and by the time you take the third step, you are on four feet as a hare. And just before you turn to run, you see Cerridwen transform into a greyhound and come straight for you. But even as you run, a part of you is observing the solidity of the earth beneath your feet. You run over the grass, which has fed you and will in turn be fed by you when this body dies. You begin to understand the perfection of the cycle in which you find yourself. It is a gift to eat and be eaten.

But now the Lady is very near and you come to the edge of the river and dive in, only to become a slick, quicksilvery salmon. The water moves around you and you move through it. You are held on all sides, supported from below, from above, front and back, side to side. There is only the barest hint of resistance from the water, but you move through it easily. And as you move through it, you find understanding beginning to grow in you. It is a gift to shape and be shaped by your world.

At the same time you recognize that Cerridwen has become a hungry-for-salmon otter. You double your pace but she is getting closer when you come to the top of the water and take off into the air. You become a wren.

You hear a shrill cry as the Lady transforms once again and chases you in the form of a hawk. You feel the air under your wings, and you are pushing against it and you are so light and you rise into the sky. You begin to see the clarity, the beauty, and you send forth your song. You find yourself contemplating the mystery. It is a gift to take in your world and give voice to it.

But, lest we forget, Cerridwen is still after you! Again, relying on your growing power, you fly back to the yard where this all began. You see the pile of golden corn strewn about for the chickens and something tells you, "The seed; you must become the seed." And as you hit the ground, you find yourself in the form of a brilliant yellow kernel of corn, the seed within the dry fruit. And for a moment, you rest.

You rest from the panic, the fear. You rest from the deepening of understanding that comes from your experience. These lessons, everything you have done and seen and been up to this moment comes to rest, encased within this seed. In the quiet darkness, you integrate; you digest . . .

––––––––––

Again, this story could go on and on, but we will stop here.

Take some time to write about your experience with your transformative powers. This story was told from the perspective of the child who is changed. Consider how it might be different for the goddess herself, or the blind fire tender! Or even another bird or fish who watched the transformations and thought, *what is this?*

––––––––––

These are only examples of what is possible in the Library. These stories may speak deeply to you, or you may find yourself digging through your own bookshelves to find the tales you love best. And don't forget that the Library has a nonfiction section! Fall in tragic love reading letters from Oscar Wilde to Lord Alfred Douglas. Stand firm at the Battle of Yorktown. Find courage in the story of Ruby Bridges.

You will have your own favorite tales that entice and delight you, and all may be found here.

More Magick at the School

The School is a good place for workings that involve brainpower, or when you need to get advice from the smartest and most talented minds that have ever existed.

A Spell for Clarity and Wisdom

HERE'S WHAT YOU NEED:

A white candle

A pin or knife for carving into the wax

Essential oil of sage or camphor (dilute!)

HERE'S WHAT YOU DO:

Think about what you are looking for and get it down to a word or a few; e.g., "clarity," "true visions," "eyes to see, mind to discern," or some suchlike phrasing.

Using the pin or knife, inscribe this into the wax of the candle, alternating with your full name (generally, you can make it fit three times around the candle).

Pour the oil into the palm of your hand, and rub your hands together to warm it and wake it up.

Dress the candle from base to wick (foot to head), repeating the phrase you've chosen to describe your desire.

Ask your gods and/or spirits to help you.

Empower the candle by whatever means you like (if you're not sure, take big, deep breaths and blow on the candle from base to wick, letting your breath charge the wax).

Light the candle and give it your attention as it draws up the wax into the wick.

Leave it to burn in a safe place until it goes out by itself.

As always, making a connection with the candle, the knife, and the oil before the working will lend much more energy!

The Council of Elders

In your journey to the School, you may have met with wise teachers. Now it's time for you to tap that resource to get assistance with a personal question.

First, have in mind what you want help with. It's good to know what you want before calling a bunch of busy people together!

Next, breathe your way into your Sanctuary, and from there to the School. Find the Council Room and take a seat. From here, send out the call to those who you think might be able to help. Need inspiration for your writing? How about inviting the Inklings: C. S. Lewis, J. R. R. Tolkien, and the lesser known Charles Williams? Or are you looking for some insight into the intersection between science and spirituality? Bring on board Carl Sagan or Francis Collins or Sir Francis Bacon. Maybe what you are looking for is a more well-rounded answer to a personal conundrum, and JFK, David Bowie, and Josephine Baker have just the kind of minds (and moves!) you need.

Tell these wise, talented, eccentric, creative, and curious folks about your problem and ask their help. Depending on who your councilors are, it could get quite boisterous and turn into a party. But perhaps you are more inclined toward the Dalai Lama, Gandhi, and Thich Nhat Hanh, in which case your council might be a delightfully silent affair.

Spend as much time as you'd like with your council. When you feel you have a good solution, give thanks to your guests and depart this sacred space.

Crown of Success Spell

Here's a favorite spell for success in your endeavors, scholarly or otherwise.

HERE'S WHAT YOU NEED:

Sage essential oil

Bay essential oil

A yellow candle

A pin or knife to inscribe the candle

HERE'S WHAT YOU DO:

Inscribe your name lengthwise on the candle three times, leaving space between.

Inscribe your desire for success in just a few words; e.g., "making top grades" or "solving the equation" or "moving through writer's block" between the inscriptions of your name.

Dress the candle by pouring the oils (diluted, please!) into your hands and rubbing them into the candle from base to wick. Recognize that you are infusing your desire into this candle.

When you are finished, light the candle and pay special attention to the moment when the wick brings up the wax.

Let it burn down in a safe place.

Blessed be your success!

Part Three

THROUGH THE
GATES OF MAGICK

Nine

THE WILDERNESS
WITHIN YOU

You have now visited the places of humanity in the secret country, the institutions that serve the need or desire for a home, dark and bright, and for spiritual communion and education. All these are driven by humanistic concerns.

But there are places in the secret country that are not that. There are places that exist independent of civilization. Though they are within you, they reflect the great wildernesses of the world. Here you explore the kingdoms of nature: the classical elemental realms of earth, air, fire, and water.

Of course, we now know that there are at least 115 elements in the periodic table, but it is helpful to use this simpler framework, traditional to many magickal systems, to guide this part of the journey

In these places, you connect with the aspects that make each element unique. If you are Pagan (or even if you're not), you might already have a practice that includes these forces. If you don't, I welcome you to discover a new relationship with the physical world.

Earth and air, fire and water, are all required for the continued existence of life as we know it. They have something to teach you, and they have spirits native to those habitats who you can meet to learn deeper truths about how you interact with these worlds, inner and outer.

You will see that the elemental kingdoms are manifest in the shared reality. Every day you touch them. The dirt below your feet and the food you eat, the atmosphere of our planet and the breath you take in, the great seas of the world and the blood in your veins, the lightning storm and the firing of neurons that carry your thoughts across the universe of your brain: all these things are related to each other. They remind you that you belong here, that you are integral to the complicated workings of life on Earth.

Starhawk describes the "Declaration of the Four Sacred Things" in her novel *The Fifth Sacred Thing*:

> The earth is a living, conscious being. In company with cultures of many different times and places, we name these things as sacred: air, fire, water, and earth.
>
> Whether we see them as the breath, energy, blood, and body of the Mother, or as the blessed gifts of a Creator, or as symbols of the interconnected systems that sustain life, we know that nothing can live without them.

The Blessing of Your Senses

I invite you now to take a moment and think of the warmth of the sun on your face. Take a breath for that feeling. Think of a sweet-smelling breeze cooling you. Breathe that in. Hear the calming trickle of flowing water. Breathe in that sound. All these things are supported by and held to the solid earth. Breathe for the dirt below your feet.

Of course there is a purely physical aspect to these explorations. If all you did was sit on the bank of a river and pay attention to the flow, you would see many lessons there: to go around when you can't go through, to wear down by persistence when force doesn't work. You are a creature of this Earth, including your brilliant mind. You can observe events and processes in nature and look for the correspondences to your daily life in the shared reality.

Of the Three Souls, the Fetch is the closest to and most connected with the physical form and the physical elements themselves. Through Fetch, you feel yourself as the beast you are and take your place in the family of fur and feather. Only slightly more complicated than other animals, Fetch is as desirous of comfort and as enchanted by the beauty of the physical realm as any other child of nature.

Fetch is at home with the elements and understands them on a visceral level. The five senses of the flesh give you the capacity to know your place in the world, in the moment. Also, through these gates of sensation, you can hear laughter and birdsong, watch the sunrise over the ocean, taste the sweet tang of an orange. You can feel the penetrating warmth of the sun and smell the roses in the garden.

Understanding and connecting with animal and plant forms is one of the gifts of the Fetch. The more you are centered in this part of you, the more easily you can relax into those relationships.

Fetch also gets attached to people or things through threads of energy that you are constantly creating. Those ties are strengthened and become closer and larger through attention. Thus, you form your universe, so it's important to be conscious of what you focus on. Fetch will naturally send more energy down threads leading to things that are attractive or inspiring, if you let them. A healthy and trusting Fetch will draw to you things of beauty and power.

How to build that trust?

As with all things, it's important to just listen. Make time to understand. It is not easy. Sometimes trying to figure out what Fetch wants is like trying to figure out what Lassie is trying to say: has Timmy really fallen into the well? Fetch can respond using the pendulum for yes-or-no questions or more complicated questions, if you are clever in how you picture the different options. Fetch speaks through applied kinesiology, the art of allowing one's body to respond to different substances (for instance, possible allergens). Dream work, meditation, automatic collage, painting, or drawing are all good ways of letting Fetch have a say.

Fetch responds to love and care, just like any other creature. So, no more cursing yourself with negative mind-talk! Change "I'm an idiot!" to "How can I fix this?"

Think about your beast-self. Speak to them with kindness. Be nice. Give them a name that only you know and let them know to not listen to one who doesn't know that name. Walk on the beach, cuddle in blankets, and eat ice cream or broccoli, have luxurious sex, get a massage. Whatever you do, make your physical pleasure the priority. Mary Oliver, in her poem "Wild Geese," writes, "You only have to let the soft animal of your body love what it loves..." and this is not just a good idea. It is a charge. I would say that for optimum health, you *must* let your body love what it loves.

There is also an esoteric aspect to the wilderness. There are great magicks at work in the precise step of a spider or an eagle's unerring vision. There is a profound wisdom in the connection of animals to their environment. The smells, sights, and sounds are a language that speaks directly of what has gone, what is here now, and what is coming. You are much more capable of understanding this language than you probably consider yourself.

And, you can go in a different direction than biology and try on different magickal systems to see if they fit. You can investigate how the ancients framed the powers of these elements and see if there is something there for you.

In some schools of thought, the elements are assigned to the four points of the compass: air in the east, fire in the south, water in the west, and earth in the north. Though these correspondences may change because of your specific geography (it makes no sense to turn your back to the ocean to call on the powers of water!), for now this is where you begin.

The elements also map to the four pillars of magickal success. Air teaches you to know; fire, to will. From water, you learn to dare, and from earth, to keep silent. Each of these powers serves a purpose in the evolution of a spiritual being. We will dig further into this as we go along.

All sorts of entities make their homes in the elemental realms and they are well-suited to helping you navigate those places and those lessons. Some of these creatures have counterparts in the shared reality, and when you develop a relationship with one of these, you have a responsibility to attend to how they fare in the world of ranchers and hunters. Wolves and eagles (and many other animals) are in danger from habitat loss and bad conservation laws. There are organizations working to save these wild populations. If you would have these as allies, it's best to do your part in both worlds.

There are also beings you will meet who are almost never seen in the physical realm. You might consider these as nature spirits, elementals, or archetypes of an energetic pattern. These entities go by different names in different traditions, sometimes simply "elementals of air" or "spirits of air." I like the term "Wildfolk," coined by Katherine Kerr in her Deverry series.

And so, you begin this next part of the journey through the secret country of yourself with a profound awareness of yourself as a physical being. You walk the path of the ancients, the priests and priestesses of the old ways, to find your own unique track to your own unique truth. Be welcome and know yourself kin with all you meet here in these most magickal realms of air, fire, water, and earth.

The Realm of Air: The High Mountains

The Gift of Knowing

You begin in the east, the direction of sunrise and the spring, of new beginnings and the freshening of all things. East is the direction of air, the first utterance of the gods as they took their initial breath in the world. You visit air to learn about communication and inspiration.

In this realm you see how things look so very different from on high. You explore the spaces between things, from atoms to universes, to the vast distance between my mouth and your ear. You go to the mountains. Fly with the birds. Stand on the highest point and let the air move through you and around you.

Air fills the space that isn't full of something else. It carries the delightful sound of children's laughter or the fearful sound of screaming, the scent of flowers or garbage. Air doesn't judge; it is the ever-objective messenger. Breath is in the realm of this element, and all things breathe.

Because it carries sound and blows away hazy thoughts, air is the element of clarity, speech, and poetry. The word "inspiration" means, of course, the awakening into action, but it also means, literally, to breathe in, and this gives you some idea of how easily this gift may be available: as easy as our natural rhythm of respiration.

There are many ways to feel the gifts of air. Because this gracious element is all around you, and you have had a relationship with it since your very birth (as you have with all of the elements), simply focusing on the breath begins the process of connection. This is a reflexive process that you are also somewhat in control of; you can change the rhythm and depth of your breath, though you can't stop yourself from breathing enough to keep you alive!

The pillar of the east, of air, is to *know*, and this is the beginning of all magicks. Study is part of this step, but only part. Knowing encompasses much more than book learning; it requires a deeper level of integration and understanding about its subject, but also about oneself.

The tool that holds the power of air is the knife. You may have a knife or athame on your altar already. If not, now would be a good time to find the perfect-for-you blade.

To represent air on the altar, you might use feathers or incense. The movement of air from a fan can be thought of as removing clouds from your mind, and thus helping you to see clearly what is important. The color associated with air is yellow or sometimes pale blue.

In the realm of air, the birds are king. You may meet the eagle or the wren, the pelican or the peacock. What these beings have in common is that they can transcend the earth for periods of time, which gives them a unique view on life. Things look small from up there!

The elementals of air are flighty (of course) and easily distracted. None are better at carrying a message, though, if you can set it within them to go in a straight line from your mouth to another's ear. This is helpful when you need to communicate at a distance.

Visiting the Realm of Air

Let's go now and explore the high mountains of the air realm.

Begin with the breath. Let the breath you take in fill you and feed you. Let the breath you take in invigorate the cells of you and between the cells, the emptiness that is you. Breathe into your center, into that still point within you, that place of restful, peaceful calm. Breathe into that place and let it expand around your consciousness.

Find yourself in your Sanctuary. Take a moment to relax here.

Now call on your guides and guardians, if you like, to come and be with you on your journey.

When you are ready, leave your Sanctuary and go around to the east. There is a faint yellow glow that emanates in a line through the rocks. This is your invitation to travel the ways of air.

There are snowcapped mountains in the distance. The path is rough and rocky. In some places it's just pea gravel and the path seems well tended, if a bit unforgiving. In other places the path leads right over boulders or through the center of massive outcroppings that seem to have burst forth from the earth just moments ago.

There is nothing green growing, only moss on the rocks. The day is cold and gray. The only living things you see are birds, high in the air. This is not a welcoming environment, but you are welcome here.

Suddenly, you come to a great hill, tufted with sparse grasses. The wind is strong. Feel it snap at your clothing and your hair. The light that beckoned you from your Sanctuary still glows toward the top of the hill, but the wind pushes you back. It will be a struggle to continue, but you press on. Soon, you are leaning so far into the wind that you are nearly horizontal.

Finally, it becomes too dangerous. Find a sheltering rock and wrap your cloak more firmly around you. Look out over the land. You can see your Sanctuary from here, you can see everything... there is the ocean, the desert, the forest.

So much of the world is sky; it reaches as far as you can see. The wind sculpts the waves of the sea, shapes the trees in the forest, and curves the sand of the desert. Such power! Such immense strength in this invisible force! Soon, the sun goes down, the tempest calms, and you can rest.

You awaken to find the first pale light of dawn breaking. Everything seems fresh and new, the very first, the original of itself, crisp and clean. Take a deep breath. Allow the yellow glow that showed you the way here to fill you as you breathe. Feel the heaviness of your body begin to lighten. Feel your molecules release their hold on each other. Soften. Rise.

Let yourself take the shape of a bird, whatever sort comes to mind. Feel the beat of your wings as you direct yourself here and there.

Hear a kind voice offering a greeting. Allow the source of that voice to become visible to you, whatever it looks like: a sparrow, a kestrel, a woodpecker? Some other spirit, unrecognizable to you?

Spend some time here, connecting to this spirit. Perhaps over time they will become an ally.

Wander for a bit. Give yourself time to become familiar with the currents of air, warm and cold, quick and soft.

Remember, you can return here whenever you wish, so there is no need to rush.

When you are ready to depart, offer gratitude to the air here in the high mountains.

Head back to your Sanctuary.

Take some time to sit for a bit with your experience. If you have gathered anything on your trip, find a place for it.

Take a seat when you are ready and come back to the breath.

Let the breath you take in fill you and feed you. Let the breath that you take in invigorate the cells of you and between the cells of you. Follow your breath into your body ... and out. And in ... and out. And once more, follow your breath into your body and back out into the space of light and noise, the shared reality. And when you are ready, open your eyes and be here now.

Air—Head, Heart, Hands
HEAD: FACTS ABOUT AIR

- Work on the questions from your travelogue pages, adding in these specific to the realm of air:

  How do you clear your mind?

  How do you tend to deal with adversity? Push forward? Back down? Why?

- Write about a time when you persevered through great difficulty and found freedom on the other side.

- Research the clean air laws in your state or region.

HEART: AIR, MOVE US

- Sing your prayers.

- Do this breathing meditation: Let your breath be in whatever rhythm it wants, whatever depth it wants. As you exhale, envision a haze of confusion, dis-ease, discomfort coming forth on your breath. Take a moment at the end of your exhalation to feel your body's desire for air. As you inhale, envision a clarifying light entering your body. Again, take a moment to hold at the top of your inhalation to feel your body's desire to breathe out and complete the cycle. Do this for as long as you like!

HANDS: AIR FEEDS YOU

- Lie on your back and gaze at the sky. Let your eyes focus only on what has no connection to the Earth. If you can, remove from your field of vision anything that is rooted to the ground.

- When you see a bird flying, follow it with your eyes. Let the swoop and dip of their flight take place in your own body. Let yourself embody the freedom of a bird in flight, no boundaries, swimming through air.

- Locate the high mountains on your map.

The Realm of Fire: The Desert of Shifting Sands
The Gift of Will

Now you turn to the south, the direction of noon and summer, of heat and light. Fire transforms; it is the only element that is actually a process: the phenomenon of combustion manifested in light, flame, and heat. Fire turns ice to water, water to steam. It takes the visible and makes it invisible. In its presence, what is still becomes excited, literally, as molecules hop around in being heated.

Fire's gift is the ability to consume fuel and bring action from stillness. Anything that is exposed to fire responds to it, just as you respond to energy stimulation in other settings. There is a reason that we talk about a situation heating up: the application of fire causes greater movement, more activity: passions arise, feelings twist and shift, things disappear and reappear with a quickness.

The pillar of the south, of fire, is to *will*, and this is the energy that ignites air's idea and makes it glow. Your ability to move out into the world with your ideas, to power through difficulties and to change things to your liking are gifts of fire. It's important to be thoughtful about your use of will and of fire so you only destroy the things you mean to. It's easy for both to get out of hand.

The magickal tool that holds the power of fire is the wand (or the flaming torch). The wand directs energy, spreading light and heat. A wand may be made of wood, crystal, metal, or glass. Each of these materials will impart some of their own quality into the tool: wood indicates growth and natural processes; crystal wands may be loving, grounding, or sober, depending on what stones are used. A copper wand is a great conductor and glass is fragile, but very clear. You might like to keep a wand on your altar as well for directing energy and stimulating growth.

To represent fire on the altar, you might use anything that gives heat or light: an interesting lamp, oil lantern, or candle. Fire's transformative power is excellent for burning a symbol of something you want rid of (really just changing it into a different form). In the tarot, the suit of Wands is the suit of fire and has to do with action and energy. The colors of fire are red and orange.

In the realm of fire, you may meet the lion who carries the flame in her heart, or the lizard who relies on the heat of the sun to keep it alive. In any case, the lessons of fire are that it can (a) keep you alive, or (b) kill you. A dangerous, but most helpful, ally.

The elementals associated with fire are sometimes frantic, often spinning and spinning in the flames, beyond hot. They are present in all forms of fire, from the forest fire to the candle that lights your way. They add vitality and illumination to any situation.

Visiting the Realm of Fire

It's time now to go and explore the shifting sands of the desert of fire.

Begin with the breath. Let the breath you take in fill you and feed you. Let the breath you take in invigorate the cells of you, and between the cells, the emptiness that is you. Breathe into your center, into that still point within you, that place of restful, peaceful calm. Breathe into that place and let it expand around your consciousness.

Find yourself in your Sanctuary. Relax for a moment. Invite your allies to be with you if you wish.

Leave your place, and head off to the south. The path shines with a red glow. This is your invitation to travel the ways of fire. This path is bare and the soil feels dry under your feet. As you continue, it becomes sandy. The warmth of the sand is comfortable. You can almost feel your blood moving faster as the cells of you heat up.

As you walk, feel the heat from above and below. The sun shines down on you, warmth rises from the sand, and soon it becomes oppressive. Look around to see yourself surrounded by sand dunes, curving and stretching in all directions. You become feverish. You are thirsty, but there is no water. You sweat and sweat until you are empty of any moisture. You can go no farther. Feel the weakness of your limbs and let your body collapse. Close your eyes and see the red behind your eyelids, then darkness. Everything seems to disappear, your pain, your fear, your anger. Recognize that when you empty yourself entirely, you are filled with the energy of the universe. You become the electricity that leaps across the synapses of your mind. Let yourself go, into your own flesh, into your own blood, then further in, to where the cells of you connect to each other, and the molecules of you. Go into where the spontaneous leap of lightning from one neuron to another is all that you can feel. This is the energy of your deepest internal process, the spark that drives your heart to life, the power and potential that ignites all things. You are consumed. Night falls.

Now open your spirit-eyes and see a group of people huddling around. You are the small fire in the center of their circle. You dance and flicker with the flames.

Someone brings more wood and you are so very hungry! You consume the logs as fast as they bring them and grow larger and larger. Soon the people are removing outer garments, beginning a merry dance around you.

You hear echoes of the realm of air in the playing of the pipes.

Someone else brings food to cook at the edge of your embers. The people are happy, warmed and fed by fire.

Now allow your consciousness to withdraw from the flames, carrying within you the red light that led you here. Find your spirit body able to easily move around this desert environment.

Wander the desert for a bit. Explore. Call to you one of the denizens of this place. Who appears? The lion or the lizard? Camel or rattlesnake?

Take your time with this new friend and potential ally.

Remember, you can return here whenever you wish, so there is no need to rush.

When you are ready to depart, offer gratitude to the desert, the shifting sands. Head back to your Sanctuary.

Take some time to sit for a bit with your experience. If you have gathered anything on your trip, find a place for it here, now.

Take a seat when you are ready and come back to the breath.

Let the breath you take in fill you and feed you. Let the breath that you take in invigorate the cells of you and between the cells of you. Follow your breath into your body … and out. And in … and out. And once more, follow your breath into your body and back out into the space of light and noise, the shared reality. And when you are ready, open your eyes and be here now.

Fire—Head, Heart, Hands
HEAD: FACTS ABOUT FIRE

- Work on the questions from your travelogue pages, adding in these specific to the realm of fire:

  Do you have a fear of fire? A fascination?

  What in your life could use some invigoration now?

  What's your relationship with desire? How do you *want*?

  Do some research about fire. What is the hottest kind of fire? The coolest?

HEART: FIRE, TRANSFORM US

- Sit with a candle, or better yet a fire in a pit, and let yourself stare into the flames. Let your vision soften. You may begin to see things to come, things that have been, or you may find yourself seeing the fire spirits.

- If it is your path, do a sweat, a sauna, or even a Bikram yoga class. Let the heat clear your mind and heart.

HANDS: FIRE FEEDS YOU

- Take a candle and lighter into a dark space with you. Sit in the dark for a while. Then light the candle. Feel the gratitude for the tiny bit of warm glow.

- Let yourself get cold, then get near a heater! Fire, in some form, is present everywhere there is warmth.

- Locate the deserts on your map.

The Realm of Water: Rivers to the Sea
The Gift of Daring

Now turn to the west, the direction of twilight, of autumn, of maturity. In the west is the gate of the ancestors through which we all pass on our way to the place of rest. West is the direction of water, the embracing of relationship as a motive force. Invoke water for cleansing, dreaming, and connection.

Water flows through all things that live. It is the source of life and the universal solvent. It cleanses all things, fills all things and eventually dissolves (nearly) all things. Water is also a nurturer and a healer. A warm salt bath takes you right back to your mother's womb.

Water is a master of inclusion without losing individuation: consider the drop in the ocean. Consider each of us as a cell in the body of God, entirely ourselves, but entirely subsumed. It is easy to lose awareness of your selfhood when you realize that you are one with all; that feeling of union is seductive. But it is important to keep a sense of your singular self so that you can get on with the business of being who you are.

The heart is ruled by water: sweet love to pounding passion. The connections between partners, lovers, family, and community are part of this element. Water fills and is shaped by what contains it, and so it's best to be conscientious about what you allow to shape your heart's expression. You are the chalice and the liquid within it.

The pillar of the west, of water, is to *dare*. In this phase, you open your heart, which is the bravest practice of all: to feel in full all the possibilities of your actions. Once you take the idea and ignite it with will, you must invest it with your love. This tempers the fire and allows for greater strength.

The tool that holds this power is the chalice or the cauldron. The chalice is most often used as a drinking vessel into which you pour a magickal liquid that you will take in for refreshment or other purposes.

The cauldron is used as a holding place for those things you wish to offer up to a higher power for resolution; for instance, you might put a picture of yourself as a child into the cauldron, invoking the power of the mother to care for you.

To represent water on the altar, one would keep, well, water! In a fancy or not-so-fancy cup or chalice. You might also keep shells or rocks from the rivers or oceans, but be aware that while there are some sellers that are sensitive to these issues, many shells for purchase are not responsibly harvested and cause detriment to our waters. It's best to use what you find yourself, as always, being sensitive to the needs of the place. Also, there's a certain synchronicity in using what is put before you to find.

Water is associated with the suit of Cups in the tarot and speaks to matters of the heart. Blue and green are the colors.

In water are the creatures of sea and river, dolphin and whale, octopus and goldfish. These can teach you to move easily through the world with grace, to go around what you can't go through, and to play.

The spirits of water are languid creatures, slippery and intimate. They are present in all forms of water, from Mother Ocean to the creek behind your house. These spirits are easy to connect with but difficult to comprehend. They remind you to flow with the ease of their element through all things in your life.

Visiting the Realm of Water

It's time to go now and explore water in the rivers and the seas.

Begin with the breath. Let the breath you take in fill you and feed you. Let the breath you take in invigorate the cells of you and between the cells, the emptiness that is you. Breathe into your center, into that still point within you, that place of restful, peaceful calm. Breathe into that place and let it expand around your consciousness.

Find yourself in the Sanctuary. Rest here a moment. Invite your guides and guardians if you wish. Invite the spirit of your cup to be with you!

Now head out and walk around the outside till you see a cairn of stones with water bubbling up from the center. There is a spring beneath the rocks, and the water climbs from deep within the earth to create a stream of water that leads off to the west. Follow this stream; see how it bends and shapes light within itself. There is a faint blue glow to it. This is your invitation to travel the ways of water.

Walk beside the stream; see the flashes of light, tiny fish darting back and forth, as the channel grows in size. The bank becomes deeper and the fish larger, and soon you come to the edge of the forest. The trees come all the way down to the water and your gentle path has become impassable. The stream has become a powerful river, flowing quick and strong. The deep currents can trick you and sweep you away before you know it. But how else can you go forward?

There is a boat of sorts at the river's edge. It doesn't look too safe, but this is an adventure, after all. You climb into the boat only to notice that there are no oars, no way of managing your speed or direction. You close your eyes and pray to whatever gods will hear you that you make it safely to wherever you are supposed to be going.

The sound of the rushing water is overwhelmingly loud. The boat is rocking, and every now and then, water comes up over the edge and soaks your feet. You hold on for dear life. But soon it simply becomes tiresome to be that afraid. You begin to relax first your face, then your shoulders, then your hands on the wooden edge of the boat. As you release your death grip, you find that the rapids slow to a gentle rocking and the loud crashing of the river becomes a gentle whoosh, whoosh. *It sounds like a heartbeat pushing blood through your veins. Lie back in the boat and feel the afternoon sun on your face. Feel the river beneath you lulling you into a state of suspended imagination, your thoughts floating freely. Your heart opens. You are calm. You feel it is right to slip out of the boat and into the gentle river. You feel the blue glow of the water path flowing through you and know that the flow will take you exactly where you need to go.*

Let yourself grow into the shape of a fish or another water creature. Feel how you are embraced on all sides.

Hear a kind voice offering a greeting. Allow the source of that voice to be-
come visible to you, whatever it looks like, perhaps an otter, alligator, salmon, or
turtle? Or another that you don't recognize?

Spend some time here, connecting to this spirit. They may become an ally
over time.

Explore this river, all rivers, the seas. Remember, you can return here when-
ever you wish, so there is no need to rush.

When you are ready to depart, offer gratitude to the water from the rivers
to the sea.

Make your way to the land and head back to your Sanctuary.

Take some time to sit for a bit with your experience. If you have gathered
anything on your trip, find a place for it here, now.

Take a seat when you are ready and come back to the breath.

Let the breath you take in fill you and feed you. Let the breath that you take
in invigorate the cells of you and between the cells of you. Follow your breath into
your body ... and out. And in ... and out. And once more, follow your breath
into your body and back out into the space of light and noise, the shared reality.
And when you are ready, open your eyes and be here now.

Water—Head, Heart, Hands
HEAD: FACTS ABOUT WATER

- Work on the questions from your travelogue pages, adding in
  these specific to the Realm of Water:

  How comfortable are you submerged in water? Do you like to
  swim?

  Are you happy with your love relationships and your level of intimacy?

  What embraces you? What limits you?

- Investigate the condition of water in your area. If there are pol-
  luted waterways, is there anything you can do about it?

HEART: WATER, SHAPE US

- Sing a song of water. Sing it in the shower.

- Find a still pool or even a puddle. Let your consciousness relax. See what you may see. Consider that these could be true knowings.

- Watch the rain. Trace a single drop as it separates from its fellows and makes its own way, then returns to the larger community of water. Imagine you can still see that separate being as it frolics and dances with the others. Be willing to be that joyous.

HANDS: WATER FEEDS YOU

- To connect with the element of water, get in some! Be aware of how water parts to admit you into it. Feel how water flows over you, caressing you intimately, claiming you as kin.

- Whenever you take water into you, as coffee or as part of the Untangling Rite, be aware of water's gift of lubrication, quenching and conducting your impulses. As you drink, give gratitude for the gift of this liquid that sustains us.

- Locate the rivers and seas on your map.

The Realm of Earth: Forest and Field

The Gift of Silence

Finally, turn to the north, the direction of midnight, of winter, of old age and death. North is the direction of earth, solidifying and bringing what you've been working on into the shared reality. Invoke earth for manifestation and remembering your place in the worlds: you are fed and you are food.

Earth is the beginning and end of your physical form, literally: you come from the earth, you are nourished by the earth, you are made of earth; you return to the earth, you feed the earth, the earth is made of you. It is the hills and the trees, the food you eat and the ground you walk on, the womb that brings you forth and the tomb that welcomes you back at the end of your mortal life.

The cycles of life on our home planet are great teachers. You can plant a tomato seed and watch it break its shell and unfurl its tiny greenery in the spring. Next it grows tall and strong, relying on the minerals and nutrients it draws up from within the topsoil. Late summer brings white and yellow flowers, which, if the pollinating wind is kind, will give birth to tiny green fruit. The sun beats down and feeds the fruit with light until finally they turn red, or yellow, or purple, and are ready to eat. After the harvest, the plants die, but they've left the seeds of their next generation living in the fruit. If conditions are right, new tomatoes will grow.

Life and death and life returning.

The pillar of the north, of earth, is to keep silent. In this phase, things come fully into being (though they may not be finished, now they are manifest). Keeping silent is another way of saying "being confident." Though you may still have doubts about your work or your abilities, don't let them rule you and don't fret. When you become unsure, acknowledge the feeling, thank it for its gifts, breathe, and release it. In silence.

The tool that holds this power is the pentacle, usually inscribed on a disc of wood or metal. This symbolizes the union of all the elements into that which is ready to come into being. Put a symbol or image of what you're working toward on this disc, with a stone on it (lodestone works great for this) to help bring it forth.

Earth corresponds, of course, to the pentacles of the tarot and matters of money and the physical body. The colors are green and black.

To represent earth on the altar, one would use salt, dirt, rocks, bones, anything that is of the earth, particularly what comes from underground. Again, finding things yourself is a great way to stay conscious of your connection with this element. If you are purchasing items, try to find out where they come from.

Humans are most familiar with the realm of earth. This is our home turf, which we share with dogs and bears, elephants and kittens. All of these are our kin.

The wildfolk of earth are slowmoving, and they take care of all animals. These spirits are easiest to reach in dark places: deep forests or caverns. They are particularly fond of caves.

The challenge about connecting with the spirits of earth is that they are terribly slow moving. There may be much activity occurring, but it is often in tiny increments and occurs over a long period of time. Think of the Entmoot in *The Lord of the Rings*, where it took many days for the Ents to speak one sentence. We have to slow ourselves down considerably to experience their communication, and that can be difficult for mobile creatures!

Visiting the Realm of Earth

It's time now to go and walk the ways of forest and field.

Begin with the breath. Let the breath you take in fill you and feed you. Let the breath you take in invigorate the cells of you, and between the cells, the emptiness that is you. Breathe into your center, into that still point within you, that place of restful, peaceful calm. Breathe into that place and let it expand around your consciousness.

Find yourself in the Sanctuary. Take a moment there to get settled. Invite your guardians if you wish.

Depart your sacred space and begin walking in the direction of the north. You can recognize it by the deep green that illuminates the path. You follow the green path, kicking small rocks, reaching down to touch the grass. It's wet with dew, and insects hop away as you disturb their activities. The day is warm and lovely, and this walk is peaceful and relaxing. Soon you see before you a forest and that the path leads into the darkness. But there is still this pale green glow that guides you on, and so on you go. Following the light, you enter the woods. It is dark here under the canopy of trees, and though life springs forth from the forest floor, no sunlight touches the ground. You feel branches touch you as though they were alive. You begin to feel afraid.

Then from amidst the noises of the forest you hear a drumbeat. Let your heartbeat match the drum's beat. All of the noises here are a part of the song of the forest. Each touch on your skin is a part of the trees' eternal dance. You do belong here, a part of you knows that, even if you fear it. The pattern of the drum becomes more complex and begins moving away from you. Follow the sound.

See light sifting through the trees, and feel an answering light coming from within you. The emerald glow of the path has taken root in your being, and you are marked by your visit here. Stopping at the edge of the forest, you see rolling hills, some covered with grass, others plowed into neat rows. There are vineyards and orchards and fields of all sorts of fruits and vegetables. In this place it is clear that the partnership between land and creature, human and otherwise, is healthy and strong.

Now let yourself grow into the shape of a beast of the earth. Feel your four feet touching the ground.

Hear a kind voice, offering a greeting. Allow the source of that voice to become visible to you, whatever it looks like. A cougar or a wolf, elephant or gorilla? Maybe something else?

Spend some time here connecting to this spirit. Over time, they may become a strong ally to you.

Wander for a bit, alone or with your new friend. Give yourself time to become familiar with the lay of the land. Remember, you can return here whenever you wish, so there is no need to rush.

When you are ready to depart, offer gratitude to this place, the forests and fields and creatures here.

Head back to your Sanctuary.

Take some time to sit for a bit with your experience. If you have gathered anything on your trip, find a place for it here, now.

Take a seat when you are ready, and come back to the breath.

Let the breath you take in fill you and feed you. Let the breath that you take in invigorate the cells of you and between the cells of you. Follow your breath into your body ... and out. And in ... and out. And once more, follow your breath into your body and back out into the space of light and noise, the shared reality. And when you are ready, open your eyes and be here now.

Earth—Head, Heart, Hands
HEAD: FACTS ABOUT EARTH

- Work on the questions from your travelogue pages, adding in these specific to the realm of earth:

  Do you have any trees that are special to you?

  Is it hard for you to keep a secret?

  Have you ever tended a garden?

- Research soil composition in your neighborhood.

HEART: EARTH, HEAL US

- The earth is our mother. Can you drum her heartbeat?

- Take care of your things. Do not destroy things needlessly but only with respect, at the end of their lifespan.

HANDS: EARTH FEEDS YOU

- Go to a tree and get up close to it, lean against the rough or smooth bark, relax your body. Climb into its branches if you can and let yourself be held in the arms of this creature of Earth. Imagine you are a great cat, entirely relaxed and at ease here.

- Walk heavy, with stomping feet. Imagine that your feet are boulders, and think about the purposefulness of moving them. Rest a moment with each step. Know that when you choose it, you cannot be moved from your path.

• Locate the forests and fields on your map.

More Magick with the Elements

There are many ways to remain conscious of and connected to the elements individually, as we've talked about in the separate journeys. But there are other ways to connect with them as a whole, which adds another dimension to the interaction. Try some of these different techniques for working with the elemental energies and entities for protection, support, and fellowship.

Meeting the Elementals

This is a simple and fun journey that brings you into contact with the elemental spirits of earth, air, fire, and water. For this meditation, you will need to have a pinch of salt, a small cup of water, a lit candle, and your own sweet breath.

Breathe deeply and let the breath you take in fill you and feed you. Relax and let your vision shift, let your body relax. Feel the creature-ness of you, the brilliant mind, and the powerful god of you, three-in-one, an entity of grace and beauty.

Place the salt on your tongue: body of earth be blessed. Follow this bit of salt into you and feel your cells begin to stir in remembrance of their origin.

Now drink the water; body of water be blessed. Follow this water into you and feel your cells soften in recognition of this nurturance.

Feel the warmth of the candle; body of fire be blessed. Follow this warmth into you and feel your cells enliven with this stimulus.

Now breathe deeply; body of air be blessed. Follow this breath into you and feel your cells awaken to this inspiration.

Sit with this for a moment, feeling your kinship with the elements of life. Now allow your Sanctuary to arise around you.

From there, envision yourself leaving this room.

Move up into the hills, up into the great forest. Find yourself surrounded by immense trunks, with branches far, far from your reach. It is cool here and moist under the trees. There are sounds around you, sliding and slithering, rustling, but you are safe and protected by the great ancient beings that encircle you. Take a moment in this sacred space and prepare to see who you see.

Feel your consciousness slowing. The time of earth is so very slow. Send your awareness into the soil, just a bit. Feel the movement of this theoretically solid ground. There are sparks of light here and there, and you can feel tiny animals moving around.

Now call to those elemental spirits of earth. They are great and powerful beings, slow moving, but full of grace and deep love for their charges.

Let yourself come into their presence, if you and they will. Listen for their slow voices. Is there a message here for you? A gift of an image or a symbol?

Take a moment now to be fully in this space for this time.

Now thank these wonderful beings and withdraw from their presence.

Next, begin to hear a trickling sound, a soft flowing sound. Water is moving nearby. Move out from the trees and follow the sound of the water as it gets louder and louder until you see the shine in the moonlight where flows the river.

Find yourself a nice place on the bank, or even step into the water and let the quick movement of the river bring you back up to speed.

Feel the flow of the water around your form. Watch as it comes toward you, moves against you, goes past. Call to the elemental spirits of water. They can be capricious and have a short memory, but their power is great and they welcome those of good heart.

Let yourself come into their presence now, if you and they will. Listen for their silvery voices. Have they a message for you? An image, perhaps, or a symbol?

Take time to be fully present in this space. Now thank these delightful beings and withdraw from their presence.

Suddenly, you hear the sound of an explosion! You see that a tree has been struck by lightning and is burning at its heart. Come close to the tree and see how the flames lick all throughout the dry, hollow trunk. Feel the warmth creeping into your body. Send just a bit of your awareness into the fire and feel the movement there, the intensity.

Call to the elemental spirits of fire. They are powerful, quick moving, and hungry, but willing to work with you if they are treated with respect.

Let yourself come into their presence, if you and they will. Listen for their quick voices. Is there a message here for you? A gift of an image or a symbol?

Take a moment to be fully in this space for this time. Now thank these forceful beings and withdraw from their presence.

Let the warmth of the fire push and push you up; feel yourself rising on the night air. Let your spirit body be blown softly, like the seed of a dandelion, away from this place of heat and smoke.

You may carry the scent of sweet flowers, blowing softly over their petals, lifting the deliciousness that draws bugs and bees and other creatures to them. As air, you can travel almost anywhere you wish. You may carry a whisper or a shout, a cry of encouragement or a song of victory.

In this place of freedom and movement, call to the elemental spirits of air. They can be frivolous, but their power is great, and no one is better at carrying messages.

Let yourself come into their presence now, if you and they will. Listen for their whispery voices. Have they a message for you? An image, perhaps, or a symbol?

Take time to be fully present in this space for now. Now thank these sweet beings and withdraw from their presence.

It is time to depart this sacred space and return to your Sanctuary. If there is anything you've received on your journey, find a place for it here.

And prepare to come back to the shared reality. Take a seat and come back to the breath.

Let the breath you take in fill you and feed you. Let the breath that you take in invigorate the cells of you and between the cells of you. Follow your breath into your body... and out. And in... and out. And once more, follow your breath *into your body and back out into the space of light and noise, the shared reality. And when you are ready, open your eyes and be here now.*

Recognize that your beautiful body here is made of earth and water, fire and air.

See how you reflect the slow steadiness of earth and the sinuous grace of water. See how you reflect the hunger of fire and the lightness of air.

Know that you are a beloved child of the universe and your relationship with the elements is a gift to you and to them.

A Nighttime Prayer for Protection and Good Dreams

When my children were young, we would speak these invocations each night to keep our family and our home safe. I've also used this to good effect when I was traveling and sleeping in strange places. Once you have created a relationship with the guardians of the elements, they will always be with you.

> *Wise, Free Eagle of the East,*
> *Ruler of the Mountains and the Sky,*
> *Guardian of the Powers of Air,*
> *Keep us safe and bring us good dreams.*
>
> *Strong, Fierce Lion of the South,*
> *Ruler of the Desert and the Flame,*
> *Guardian of the Powers of Fire,*
> *Keep us safe and bring us good dreams.*
>
> *Slithering, Sinuous Serpent of the West,*
> *Ruler of the Rivers and the Seas,*
> *Guardian of the Powers of Water,*
> *Keep us safe and bring us good dreams.*
>
> *Huge, Immovable Bull of the North,*
> *Ruler of the Deepest Caverns,*

Guardian of the Powers of Earth,
Keep us safe and bring us good dreams.

Guardians all,
I invite you and invoke you.
Come, be with us this night.
Care for us as the Goddess cares for all her children.
Bless me and blessed be.

———— *Ten* ————

HOME AGAIN, HOME AGAIN

The Mysteries of Birth, Life, and Death

You have traveled so far now, from the shared reality to your own safest place, through the darkness, the communion with spirit, and the gaining of knowledge. You've gone into the wilderness, the mountains, the desert, rivers, forests, and fields. You have met those who live there, gained allies, and learned valuable lessons. You found the gifts in all those places.

Now it's time to turn toward home. From the farthest reaches of the cosmos to the deepest depths of our planet and finally back in to your own bright heart, it is time to explore the mysteries of birth and life and death.

"As above, so below," it is said. But what does that mean?

Above we find the planets spinning around their suns, exploding into being and burning away. This is birth and life and death on a cosmic scale, so vast it is almost unimaginable. New galaxies are constantly bursting forth, collapsing in on themselves, and turning inside out.

Below we live our entire lives on just one of those planets, Terra, spinning around Sol, the sun, the center of our star system. Birth and life and death look different here on an earthly level, all beings becoming themselves, then separating out into their component parts, to be used again and again in the making of trees and concrete and butterflies.

Everything that has ever been is still here in some form, coming together and moving apart in an intimate, intricate dance of contraction and expansion, immanence and transcendence.

Above, there is an exhalation that began thirteen billion years ago, spinning all things out from their center and into constant motion. We are all children of that pulse. Sooner or later we will be breathed back into our first home.

Below we come forth from the earth and grow up and into our own lives until we return to her darkness at our death. This may very well be a new birth. We really have no idea.

What we do know is that we live in a universe where, on every imaginable scale, everything is rising and falling and rising again, endlessly coming together and coming apart.

From the oneness that is at the beginning of all things to the separation and dissolution at the end, each of us walks our own individual path. The actions we take and the effects we leave behind are our footprints on the body of the world, and they show where we've been.

We become aware of the cycles of our physical, mortal bodies on this planet. Our aging is a microcosm of the Earth's seasons: birth, maturity, old age, death.

The Earth breathes out and pushes sap up into the green growing things and into all life. You rise. Later, the Earth breathes in and draws all of her energy back into herself. You fall.

All the love that flows from the heart of the earth to the heart of the universe flows through you.

This is how we orient ourselves, as children of the stars and of this single planet. This is how we know our place on the thin skin of our mother.

This is how we orient ourselves, between our past and our future.

This is how we know our time is now.

From *above*, you learn to see beyond a single lifetime. You find yourself eternal, spun in and out of existence over and over. You recognize yourself as an infinite being.

From *below*, you learn to connect deeply to your single lifetime. You find yourself mortal and learn to be in and of this world, which is so lovely, but so deadly.

From your own heart, you learn that you are needed exactly where and when you are. You learn that you are a gate between your secret country and the shared reality, and that it is up to you what you bring through.

You learn all of what makes you the only you that there ever will be. Broken. Perfect. Impatient. Beloved.

Just for a moment, let's go back to the story of the Cauldron of Cerridwen. There is a bit at the end after all the chasing where the child becomes a grain of corn and the goddess becomes a black hen. Then this happens...

Soon comes the Lady, and she eats up all the seeds; she eats you up and you don't even care. You have been through so much; a long rest feels perfect. The Lady takes you into the fertile darkness of her body, and when you come into her womb, the seed, which is you, starts to open up. You begin to grow, first a tiny tail, then arms, legs, fingers, eyes. You grow a little more and become aware of the blood flowing into you and through you, fed by the Lady. The Goddess sustains you. You grow a little more and become aware of the ba-bum, ba-bum, ba-bum *of the Lady's heartbeat, and this is your first sound-feeling: the rhythm of your Holy Mother.*

For so long you are held so tightly and so comfortably and so gently in the belly of the Lady.

In comfort and ignorance, you are held in the deepest darkness. Such exquisite nothing- and everythingness! Amazing that anyone could ever fear this blackness when it returns at the end of life.

You are complete, but powerless. You are comfortable, but without any reach beyond the walls of the womb. It is the nature of life to change; you cannot remain in stasis. The container of you always becomes too small.

You will have to be born into a different world to become what you are meant to be: a god in your own right.

One day, it's just too much; you are held too tight and things are wakening in you. They are awakening you.

A squeeze and a push and there is light. Another push and you are free, and separate, and cold. It is bright and scary, but you can stretch and move. Then warm hands are holding you. And a warm voice is speaking to you. The Lady says, "Oh, you are so beautiful, perfect, exquisite. You have been worth my every pain. You are worthy of all my teaching. And now it is time for you to go among the people and be of service to all." She kisses you and wraps you up in wool and leather and sets you adrift on the river, to go and find the rest of your story...

The Heart of the Cosmos and the Gift of Freedom

The heart of the cosmos is the farthest point in time and space that anything has ever seen. It is the birthplace common to all creatures and things, a place where some becomes one becomes none becomes all-that-is. There is a reason this is a holy mystery: it is inexplicable. It must be experienced, and even then it is not truly understood. The wild expanse of space is beyond the ken of a mortal being.

Our universe is so large that the light you see from the stars has traveled millions, sometimes billions, of years to get here. When you look up into the dome of night, you are seeing a version that is no longer exactly accurate. Even the rays from our sun, Sol, take more than eight minutes to get to the surface of the Earth.

Contemplation of the cosmos releases you from your singular point of focus and opens your perspective to the grandest possible range. Our universe is so unbelievably immense that you might feel yourself as insignificant as a smidgen of salt in the ocean.

It's entirely a matter of scale. The cosmos is the entirety of everything we know and many things we don't know. The Milky Way, which is our home galaxy, is just one of one of *billions* of others. Our solar system is just one of an unknowable number of star systems. And our Earth is just one of the planets in that system.

Let's drop down a few levels:

The state of California is an entity made of counties, each of which is an entity of its own. The counties are made of towns, and the towns are made up of people. The people are made of organs, the organs are made of cells, the cells of molecules, and the molecules of atoms.

Consider that any and all of these may have a consciousness that you can connect to.

There's no telling how far we can go, in or out, with this idea. I like to assume that there is some level of awareness at every level of being: the spirit of the Milky Way itself, my home planet and its kin, my own family and our kin. I like to be fully present to all of these.

The heart of the cosmos reminds you that, no matter how far you go, all things are one. The gift of freedom is the understanding that, in the deepest place in you, you are empty space and atoms. So is everything else.

In your simplest possible form, you are a universe full of planets.

Visiting the Heart of the Cosmos

As always, begin with the breath. Let the breath you take in fill you and feed you. Let the breath you take in invigorate the cells of you and between the cells, the emptiness that is you. Breathe into your center, into that still point within you, that place of restful, peaceful calm. Breathe into that place and let it expand around your consciousness.

Find yourself in your Sanctuary. Take a moment to center yourself here.

In your mind's eye, see the ceiling of your Sanctuary. Trace a pentacle in the air and see it opening there, like a door. Allow yourself to slowly rise up and out through that gateway. Look back at the earth as you move farther out from her. Find yourself looking at your home in the shared reality, the place your physical body sits. See that, as you go higher, individual homes become a neighborhood, neighborhoods become towns. See the shapes of the world as you rise, hills and valleys, mountain ranges. See the place where the ocean meets the shore, the curves of the continents. Identify the oceans, if you can. Observe how there aren't really any physical boundaries between towns and counties and states, only collections of homes and farms and mountains and wide open spaces.

Now turn, if you haven't already, to look out from where you are, out to infinite space. Feel how it feels to turn away from Earth, our home, and toward the rest of the universe, our greater home.

Continue to rise, until you move out from where the air lives, into the dark vacuum of space. See the tiny lights of stars that are incredibly far away, all turning around a secret heart at the very center of all things. Let your awareness hold here, in this place of mystery, at the edge of what is known and unknown. Or maybe you'd like to continue on a bit farther. Do as you will, but don't forget to breathe.

Are there any beings here that you are aware of? Let yourself be still and quiet and see what you might find. You may become aware of the souls of the planets or the strange and wondrous creatures that inhabit them, or something else entirely, known only to you.

Take some time to explore.

Now it's time to move back toward our Earth. If you have made contact with any beings here, thank them for their presence as you begin to move back down into the place of air where your body breathes. Move down till you can see the shapes of the land, till you can recognize the place where your body sits. Come closer still to the physical earth. Come down past the tops of trees and into your body again. Rest here a moment in your Sanctuary.

If you have found anything on your travels, find a place for it now. And prepare to leave this sacred space.

Follow your breath into your body ... and out. And in ... and out. And once more follow your breath into your body and back out into the space of light and noise, the shared reality. And when you are ready, open your eyes and be here now.

The Heart of the Cosmos—Head, Heart, Hands
HEAD: THE BIG BANG

- Work on the questions from your travelogue pages, adding in these specific to the heart of the cosmos:

   How does thinking about the immensity of the universe make you feel?

   Have you ever had memories of other lives?

   What does our current scientific understanding tell us about the start of our universe?

- Do some research on quantum physics.

HEART: THE GODSELF OF THE UNIVERSE

- Sit outside at night and watch the sky spin, remembering that it is the rotation of the Earth that gives us this changing perspective.

- Listen to Gustav Holst's orchestral suite called *The Planets*.

HANDS: DANCING THE LIMITLESS

- Make a model of our galaxy, like you used to do in elementary school, using balls or fruit or some other round objects.

- Arrange a dance with some friends, where each of you is a planet and you rotate around one person who is the sun. Change places so everyone gets to be the center of our solar system.

- Does this place belong on your map? Is there a way to represent this?

The Heart of the World and the Gift of Form

The heart of the world is the teacher of contraction, of withdrawing into one's individual self. Here is where we come when we choose to take on a fleshly body and submit to the rigors of physical reality. We attach ourselves to this being called Earth, and from then on we are sustained by her body.

One of my favorite quotes on this subject comes from Flora Thompson's *Lark Rise to Candleford*: "A little later, remembering man's earthy origin, 'dust thou art and to dust thou shalt return,' they liked to fancy themselves bubbles of earth. When alone in the fields, with no one to see them, they would hop, skip and jump, touching the ground as lightly as possible and crying 'We are bubbles of earth! Bubbles of earth! Bubbles of earth!'"

You have come from the stars. You are made of stars. When you come here into life on Earth, you know that someday you will die. But until that day, you get to play and learn and sing and grow with others. When you were one with all things, you couldn't do that.

You submit to life as a singular self and with that, mortality. Only oneness is eternal. The singular must always die, to be taken apart and used for something else; *solve et coagula*.

We choose separation so that we may come together in different combinations and forms over and over again, in spirit-bodies or physical ones. We hold ourselves apart like two magnets so we can feel the force of desire that draws us together. Magick happens in that dynamic place.

Remember that you are a spirit, making a conscious choice to take on the limitations of form, giving up some measure of freedom, so that you can enjoy what mortal life has to offer: a rare steak, a deep kiss, an excellent wine. Without your body, there is no scent of flowers, no feeling of skin on skin.

I love the dirt life, with the spit and blood and babies and dogs. I love the laughter and the dancing. But I have watched a friend's spirit rising over the land she adored, as she was freed of the bonds of her broken flesh, and such joy I've never seen before or since. Clearly there is something very good awaiting us after we lose these chains.

My personal belief is that when we leave here, we meet up with our best beloveds on the other side. There are huge hugs all around, some tears. We might hold each other at arm's length and say, *Well, look how you've grown! I've missed you so much.*

We go to our other home, where the rest of our spirit family are all sitting around with bowls of popcorn and tasty beverages, waiting to watch the story of our life. As the images scroll by, there are gasps of surprise, angry exclamations, tears of joy and pain. Hopefully there are also fits of hysterical laughter. And when it's over, there is silence for a moment. Then *Wow! What a crazy trip! So what's next?* Then we decide whether we want to hang out or come back to Earth for another round. Maybe it feels like getting off a scary roller coaster and then choosing to ride *again, again!* Maybe a few folks agree to take the next ride together.

Truly, death is scary, because no one really knows what awaits us. But I hope that when my time comes, I will remember that death is a door that I must pass through to return to my other home.

Visiting the Heart of the World

Let us begin with the breath. Let the breath you take in fill you and feed you. Let the breath you take in invigorate the cells of you and between the cells, the emptiness that is you. Breathe into your center, into that still point within you, that place of restful, peaceful calm. Breathe into that place and let it expand around your consciousness.

Find yourself in your Sanctuary.

Trace a pentacle there on the floor and see it opening like a door. Step through and allow your awareness to sink down and through to the soil. Let yourself move

in the cold darkness past the waiting worms, through the infinitely slow move-
ment of decay, which is the beginning of dirt. Know that this dirt is made up of
many things that once walked the surface of the planet, whose molecules now are
being redistributed for reuse: bones and leaves and feathers and flesh.

There is air within the earth, and water. These have their own cycles of rising
and falling. Move down and into any open spaces you find, or rivers flowing un-
derground, wet places or dry or hard with rocks. Move down and down until you
begin to feel the heat radiating from the molten core of the Earth. Turn around,
if you will it, and look back up through the layers of soil that make up the crust
of the Earth's surface. All that you've ever seen and known of our home planet is
just a tiny layer of her outer shell. Come to the edge of the place where the rock
becomes liquid with the great force of heat and pressure. Let your awareness hold
here, in this place of mystery, at the edge of all that is known and unknown.

Are there any beings here that you are aware of? The milieu of molecules that
have coalesced at this great depth may have personalities you can connect to, or
perhaps you have found the spirit of an underground cavern or a river. You may
even become aware of something that resides in the roiling melted mass that sur-
rounds the very center of the planet. A fire elemental, huger than any other! Let
yourself be still and quiet and see what you find.

Take some time to explore.

Prepare to come back from this space, to the Earth you know. If you have
made contact with any beings here, bid them farewell as you begin to rise and
rise, through the layers of the crust of the earth, past caverns and rivers and dark-
ness, up and up, to where you begin to recognize the soil of home, up and up past
all the creatures of darkness going about their lives in their own world. Come up
and up to the floor, and then up through it, and into your own form.

Take some time to sit for a bit with your experience. If you have gathered
anything on your trip, find a place for it here, now. And when you are ready,
prepare to depart this sacred space.

Let the breath you take in fill you and feed you. Let the breath that you take
in invigorate the cells of you and between the cells of you. Follow your breath into

your body...and out. And in...and out. And once more, follow your breath into your body and back out into the space of light and noise, the shared reality. And when you are ready, open your eyes and be here now.

The Heart of the World—Head, Heart, Hands
HEAD: MILES OF DIRT

- Work on the questions from your travelogue pages, adding in these specific to the heart of the world:

  What are your beliefs about the death of the body?

  What are your funeral plans?

- Find out what lies between the ground you walk on and the center of the planet.

HEART: THE SOUL-FIRE OF THE WORLD

- Invite a dream about your death.

- Write a poem about the power of contraction.

HANDS: EVERYTHING IS FED BY WHAT CAME BEFORE

- Make a figure with sticks and name it something you are ready to release. Bury it beneath a tree and ask that the tree help it to decompose and become something useful.

- Is there a way to locate this on your map?

The Heart of You and the Gift of Yourself

The heart of yourself is your singular emanation into the milieu of everything. You come home to yourself, and you are your own home. Like any weary traveler, you see the place with new eyes. Maybe it looks very different: the berries are ripening, the roses are blooming. Maybe it is only your perception that has changed. Hopefully you have gained a new appreciation for how precious you are.

Here you remember that you are the guardian at the gate. You are the entrance point of all things from the secret country into your world. You are the beginning and end, the alpha and omega of your universe, the center and the circumference.

You are a being of power, and you bring into being the world that suits you and your fellow creatures, a world that aligns with the principles of compassion, discernment, joy, and creativity.

This is your gift and your charge: to live in accordance with your own divine will and also in harmony with the other powerful entities who are doing the same.

Visiting the Heart of Yourself

Again, begin with the breath. Let the breath you take in fill you and feed you. Let the breath you take in invigorate the cells of you, and between the cells, the emptiness that is you. Breathe into your center, into that still point within you, that place of restful, peaceful calm. Breathe into that place and let it expand around your consciousness.

Find yourself in your Sanctuary.

From this place, you may reach up or down, within or without. You may touch the universal consciousness of deep space, or the singular intensity of the core of the Earth. You may call for what you desire, or answer the call of the gods to you. You may reach out to the elements of life—earth, air, fire, and water, in their own realms and know yourself as one with them, capable and necessary. This is your point of connection with all things, your own sweet self, the heart of power beating within you, moving and changing your world as you will it, with the highest ethics and greatest drive. This is the center, which is the circumference of all, worlds within you and without. Blessed be you, beloved child of the earth and sky.

Now, once more, let the breath you take in fill you and feed you. Let the breath that you take in invigorate the cells of you and between the cells of you. Follow your breath into your body ... and out. And in ... and out. And once more, follow your breath into your body and back out into the space of light and noise, the shared reality. And when you are ready, open your eyes.

Be here now.

More Magick from the Heart

Child of Earth and Sky Practice

Stand tall.

Feel a string attached at the crown of your head. Feel it lifting your head away from your shoulders. Let your shoulders be still. Breathe.

Feel the weight of your body on your feet. Let the soles of your feet expand and truly be in contact with the floor. Wiggle your toes. Breathe.

Feel the sky's pull, encouraging you to lift your head, ever so gently, and as it lifts, to also draw up your spine, making space between the vertebrae. Feel your spine lift away from your pelvis, and your pelvis away from your legs. Feel your thighs lift from your knees, your knees from your ankles. Let there be space in all of your joints.

Feel the strength of the earth's pull on your feet, how solid her body. She will never let you go. And yet, you move about with ease, your feet lifting, one at a time, and coming back down to center on your path.

Feel the flow of life-force throughout your body. You are the point of dynamic tension between earth and sky. A child of them both. Breathe.

A Circle of Safety for Self or Stuff

Here is an easy form of a safety spell for you, your home, and your possessions. In this practice, you are drawing on the powers within yourself and connecting to the powers without.

Breathe deep. Allow your attention to come to rest in your belly. Let each breath you take in center you more firmly in yourself.

Visualize a sphere forming around you, around all that you want to keep safe. Breathe into that sphere and let its surface become strong.

Now see a light growing in your center. Let it be sparked to life by your own soul-fire and get brighter and brighter with each breath.

See the light becoming more focused, the edges becoming more discrete. Now send a root from this light into the earth.

This root will connect you to the power of the Heart of the Earth, grounded and sure.

See the root pulsing with light and potential. Breathe.

Now send another bit of that light up into the sky above you, like a lattice-work of branches.

These branches will connect you to the Heart of the Cosmos, expansive and free.

Feel yourself as the balance point of these powers. Breathe.

Now turn toward the east. Put your left hand on your heart and your right out in front of you, palm out.

Remember the yellow glow that accompanied you on your travels to the realm of air. Find it again within you and send a shaft of that light out from your hand. See it splash as it hits the inside of the sphere you created. Watch it cover the whole eastern quadrant of the circle.

Bring your hands together in front of you, releasing your hold on the shaft of light. Nod a respectful greeting to the powers of the east.

Turn toward the south. Again, left hand on heart and right out in front, palm out.

Remember the red glow that showed you the way to the realm of fire. Find that within you and send a shaft of red light out from your hand. Again, see it splash as it hits the inside of the sphere you created. Watch it cover the whole southern quadrant of the circle.

Bring your hands together in front of you, releasing your hold on the shaft of light. Nod a respectful greeting to the powers of the south.

Now turn toward the west. Again, put your left hand on your heart and your right out in front of you, palm out.

Send a shaft of the blue light you found in the realm of water out from your hand and see it splash as it hits the inside of the sphere you created. Watch it cover the whole western quadrant of the circle.

Bring your hands together in front of you, releasing your hold on the shaft of light. Nod a respectful greeting to the powers of the west.

Now turn toward the north. Put your left hand on your heart and your right out in front of you, palm out.

Send a shaft of that earthen green light out from your hand. See it splash as it hits the inside of the sphere you created. Watch it cover the whole northern quadrant of the circle.

Bring your hands together in front of you, releasing your hold on the shaft of light. Nod a respectful greeting to the powers of the north.

Now you stand in the center of a sphere of protection that has been generated by earth energy, sky energy, and your own energy, supported by the powers of the elemental kingdoms.

Draw into you whatever you might need, and release the root and branch that you've sent out from you.

Give respectful gratitudes to all.

You might like to refresh this spell weekly or monthly. If you are having a particularly difficult time in your life, add this to your morning practice.

A Song from Heart to Heart to Heart: All the Love that Flows

I wrote this chant after a dear friend shared with me the sweet blessing, *"May the love that flows between the earth and the heavens flow through you."* It goes like this:

All that love that flows from the Heart of the Earth
to the Heart of the Universe,
flows through us.
All that love that flows
from the Heart of the Earth
to the Heart of the Universe,
flows through us.
Sap is rising, rising, rising.
Sap is rising, life returns!
Sap is rising, rising, rising.
Sap is rising, life returns!

Outro

T. S. Eliot said, "We shall not cease from exploration, and the end of all our exploring will be to arrive where we started and know the place for the first time."

I hope that you have enjoyed this journey, that it has given you a tantalizing glimpse of what a treasure you are. I hope that you have been surprised and delighted and maybe just a little scared, that you've seen where you are strong and where you need help and that you've asked for that help. I hope you are awakened and renewed by your adventures in the secret country of yourself.

I said back at the beginning that everything of value in this journey was already inside of you. This has been a thorough introduction, but still it is only the start of a lifelong adventure. May you continue to seek and find your unique gifts and have the strength and courage to bring them into the shared reality.

Do not fear to fully inhabit yourself. Breathe into the center of you, your soul-fire. See that flame burning strong. Feed it breath until that fire fills all of you, from the bottom of your feet to the top of your head. Breathe once more and let the fire come out and dance where skin meets sky. Then let it subside. Feel the illumination of your power filling you, always ready to shine forth as you will.

This is you: blood and bone and bright joy.

This is you: strong and free and beautiful.

You've proven yourself in this journey. You can be proud of your achievements; no one else could have done it like you did.

May you find so many wondrous blessings wherever you go next.

Hail and farewell.

Appendix A: List of Values

Accuracy	Efficiency	Loyalty	Reverence
Achievement	Elation	Mastery	Sacredness
Acknowledgement	Elegance	Maturity	Sacrifice
Adaptability	Empathy	Meticulousness	Sagacity
Advancement	Endurance	Mindfulness	Saintliness
Adventure	Environmentalism	Modesty	Sanguinity
Aggressiveness	Excitement	Mystery	Science
Altruism	Exploration	Nature	Security
Ambition	Extravagance	Neatness	Self-control
Art	Faith	Nerve	Selflessness
Articulacy	Fame	Nonconformity	Self-reliance

Artistry	Family	Obedience	Self-respect
Assertiveness	Fascination	Open-mindedness	Sensitivity
Attentiveness	Fashion	Optimism	Sensuality
Attractiveness	Fearlessness	Order	Serenity
Awareness	Ferocity	Organization	Service
Awe	Fitness	Originality	Sexuality
Balance	Flexibility	Outdoors	Silence
Beauty	Focus	Patience	Simplicity
Benevolence	Fortitude	Passion	Sincerity
Bliss	Freedom	Peace	Skillfulness
Boldness	Friendship	Perceptiveness	Solidarity
Calmness	Frugality	Perfection	Solitude
Charity	Fun	Perseverance	Spirituality
Charm	Gallantry	Persuasiveness	Spontaneity
Clarity	Generosity	Philanthropy	Stability
Cleverness	Grace	Piety	Stillness
Community	Gratitude	Playfulness	Strength
Compassion	Growth	Pleasure	Structure
Competence	Happiness	Poise	Success
Competition	Harmony	Popularity	Sympathy

Confidence	Health	Potency	Synergy
Connection	Heroism	Power	Teamwork
Consciousness	Honesty	Practicality	Thoroughness
Consistency	Honor	Precision	Thoughtfulness
Contentment	Hospitality	Presence	Tidiness
Control	Humility	Pride	Traditionalism
Cooperation	Humor	Privacy	Tranquility
Courage	Imagination	Prosperity	Transcendence
Courtesy	Impartiality	Punctuality	Trust
Craftiness	Independence	Purity	Trustworthiness
Creativity	Individuality	Rationality	Truth
Curiosity	Influence	Reason	Understanding
Daring	Ingenuity	Recognition	Uniqueness
Dependability	Inspiration	Recreation	Unity
Devotion	Integrity	Refinement	Usefulness
Dignity	Intelligence	Reflection	Valor
Diligence	Intensity	Relaxation	Victory
Discipline	Intuition	Reliability	Virtue
Discovery	Joy	Relief	Vision
Discretion	Justice	Religiousness	Vitality

Diversity	Kindness	Resilience	Warmth
Dominance	Knowledge	Resolve	Wealth
Duty	Leadership	Resourcefulness	Willingness
Ease	Liberation	Respect	Wisdom
Ecstasy	Longevity	Responsibility	Wonder
Effectiveness	Love	Rest	Youthfulness

Exercises, Prayers, Practices, Spells, and Rites Index

Purging Preconceptions 14

The Soul-Fire Invocation 17

The Body of Talker 21

Talker Thoughts 22

The Body of Fetch 24

Feeling Fetch 24

The Body of Godself 25

Godself's Gifts 26

The Ha Prayer for Triple-Soul Alignment 28

The Untangling Rite 31

Making Your Core Values Pentacle 34

Running Your Values Pentacle 36

Unpacking the Values Pentacle 38

Making the Altar 43

Seeking the Ally 57

Talking to Your Tools 58

Ha Prayer for Integration 67

Roadblocks to Joy and Fulfillment 76

Loving-kindness Blessing Practice 79

Loving-kindness Gratitude Practice 82

Memory Play 84

Dreams and Visions Exercise 85

Cleansing Bath 87

Planting Intentions 89

Sending Energy from Godself to Godself 91

Demons vs. Shadows 98

Seeking, Hearing, Speaking 105

World Shadows 109

A Spell for Protection 109

A Talisman for Strength 110

Bone-Deep Healing 111

Your Thoughts on God 116

The Compost of Your Past 117

Trusting Your Intuition 126

The Arcane Journey 127

Cutting Ties Exercise 130

Most Powerful Allies 130

The Not-So-Silent Supper 131

Sharing Knowledge and Power 137

Thoughts vs. Thinking 144

A Spell for Clarity and Wisdom 155

The Council of Elders 155

Crown of Success Spell 156

The Blessing of Your Senses 162

Meeting the Elementals 184

A Nighttime Prayer for Protection and Good Dreams 187

Child of Earth and Sky Practice 201

A Circle of Safety for Self or Stuff 201

A Song from Heart to Heart to Heart: All the Love that Flows 203

Bibliography

Batman Begins. Directed by Christopher Nolan. Performances by Christian Bale, Katie Holmes. Warner Bros. Pictures, 2005. Film.

Cameron, Julia. *The Artist's Way.* New York: G. P. Putnam's Sons, 2002.

Captain America: The First Avenger. Directed by Joe Johnston. Performances by Chris Evans, Tommy Lee Jones, Hugo Weaving. Paramount Pictures, 2011. Film.

Carroll, Lewis. *Alice's Adventures in Wonderland.* London, England: Macmillan, 1865.

Cooper, Rabbi David. *God is a Verb.* New York: Riverhead Books, 1998.

Crowley, John. *Little, Big.* New York: Bantam, 1981.

Eliot, T. S. *Four Quartets.* San Diego, CA: Harcourt, 1943.

Freud, Sigmund. *A General Selection from the Works of Sigmund Freud.* Edited by John Rickman. New York: Anchor Books, 1989.

Kerr, Katherine. *Daggerspell.* New York: Bantam Books, 1986.

King, Serge Kahili. *Urban Shaman.* New York: Touchstone, 1990.

Kipling, Rudyard. *The Jungle Book*. New York: Century, 1920.

Lamott, Anne. *Traveling Mercies: Some Thoughts on Faith*. Waterville, MN: Thorndike Press, 1999.

Lewis, C. S. *The Lion, the Witch, and the Wardrobe*. New York: HarperCollins, 1994.

Lewis, C. S. *Perelandra*. New York: Avon Publications, 1944.

Oliver, Mary. *New and Selected Poems*. Boston: Beacon Press, 1993.

Plato. *Republic*. Translated by Desmond Lee. New York: Penguin, 2003.

Pratchett, Terry. *Small Gods*. New York: Harper, 2008.

Redmoon, Ambrose Hollingsworth. "No Peaceful Warriors," *Gnosis Magazine,* Fall 1991.

Roberts, Jane. *The Seth Material*. Englewood Cliffs, N.J: Prentice-Hall, 1970.

Rowling, J. K. *Harry Potter and the Sorcerer's Stone*. New York: Arthur A. Levine Books, 1997.

SARK. *Juicy Pens, Thirsty Paper*. New York: Three Rivers Press, 2008.

Sagan, Carl. *Cosmos*. New York: Random House Publishing, 1980.

Simone, Gail and Bernard Chang. "A Star in the Heavens, Scene 2: Personal Effects." *Wonder Woman*, Vol. 3, Number 25. New York: DC Comics, 2008.

Starhawk. *The Fifth Sacred Thing*. New York: Bantam Books, 1993.

Starhawk and Hillary Valentine. *The Twelve Wild Swans: A Journey to the Realm of Magic, Healing and Action*. New York: HarperOne, 2000.

Thompson, Flora Jane. *Lark Rise to Candleford*. London: Oxford University Press, 1957.

Tolkein, J. R. R. *The Lord of the Rings.* Boston: Houghton Mifflin, 1967.

Trungpa, Chogyam. *The Collected Works of Chogyam Trungpa: Volume Six: Glimpses of Space; Orderly Chaos; Secret Beyond Thought; The Tibetan Book of the Dead: Commentary; Transcending Madness; Selected Writings.* Edited by Carolyn Gimian. Boulder, CO: Shambhala Publications, 2010.

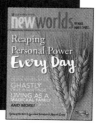

RITUALS
of
CELEBRATION

Honoring the Seasons of Life through the Wheel of the Year

Jane Meredith

Rituals of Celebration
Honoring the Seasons of Life through the Wheel of the Year
JANE MEREDITH

Create a deeper experience of the Wheel of the Year for yourself and your community. In *Rituals of Celebration,* author Jane Meredith provides lyrical accounts of the most memorable rituals she's organized, as well as how-to instructions for creating them. Inspired by Pagan, Druid, and Goddess traditions, the rituals are crafted to help us honor the changing seasons and to mark the important milestones of our personal journeys in a way that is relevant to contemporary life.

Along with the rituals, you will discover craft projects that go hand-in-hand with each festival—perfect ideas for artistic expression whether you are practicing alone, with a group, or celebrating with children. With additional instructions for building an altar and other basic tasks, this guide includes everything you need to create celebrations that will resonate deeply within you, your family, and your life.

978-0-7387-3544-3, 336 pp., 6 x 9   **$17.99**

To order, call 1-877-NEW-WRLD
Prices subject to change without notice
Order at Llewellyn.com 24 hours a day, 7 days a week!

"Respectful to tradition and relevant to the present . . .
An engaging and readable introduction to Druidry for today."
—JOHN MICHAEL GREER,
Grand Archdruid of the Ancient Order of Druids in America and the author of *The Druidry Handbook*

Penny Billington

THE PATH
OF
DRUIDRY

Walking the Ancient Green Way

The Path of Druidry
Walking the Ancient Green Way
PENNY BILLINGTON

Virtually everyone who has embarked on a spiritual path has heard of the Druids. Many have been drawn to learn more or follow their ancient practices.

The Path of Druidry teaches a clear, structured, three-strand system to help open your vision and connect to the multidimensional world understood by our Celtic forebears. It is a unique spiritual course of study grounded in the practices of modern Druids, allowing you to follow a solitary path or work with groups.

Each chapter begins with a traditional Welsh myth and includes practical exercises that help you understand the truths within these myths. But Druidry is more than just a set of practices; it is a spiritual mindset, a way of looking at yourself, the world, and your interactions with the world. Developing this mindset is the purpose of *The Path of Druidry*. It reveals how Druidry is a vital magical current you can access to deeply enrich your spiritual and daily life.

978-0-7387-2346-4, 360 pp., 7½ x 9⅛   **$19.99**
